Cats Don't Hike

To: Mom & Dad

From:

Because this book is about a family, there will be stories that sound very familiar. Rest assured, the stories are about my family, not yours. Any similarities between our stories and your stories are accidental, and the result of the fact that families have remarkably similar experiences.

Some of the observations and stories presented here concern real incidents. All names except family have been changed, or deleted entirely, to protect individual identity.

Cover art provided by Ray Keys of *The Weeklys*.

www.theweeklys.com

www.edwinleap.com

2006

Cats Don't Hike

Edwin Leap

Dedication

To Jan, Samuel, Seth, Elijah and Elysa:
Whatever I may do or be, you will always be my true calling.

Acknowledgments

I would like to thank many people for their assistance with this book, mostly my bride and best friend Jan, who is my constant editor, literary critic and computer expert. You're the best, sweetheart.

Thanks to my mom, Sharon Leap, my dad Rev. Keith Leap, and my in-laws Len and Carma Mahon, for giving me the framework of love I needed to construct my own family. I need to give a special thanks to Carma and Julie Mahon for their help in editing.

This book is a collection of columns, most of which have been featured in The Greenville News, Greenville, South Carolina. As such, I want to thank everyone at that wonderful paper that makes it possible for my words to appear on paper and to be distributed around South Carolina. It's a great honor.

Specifically, I'd like to thank retired editorial page editor Tom Inman for believing in me as a writer, and for continuing to encourage me. I also want to thank publisher Steve Brandt and current editorial page editor Beth Padgett for their ongoing confidence in me, and for the wonderful opportunity I have twice each month to rant, joke or reflect to the many readers of The Greenville News.

Thanks also to Julie Belschner, former editor, Brett McLaughlin, current editor and Jerry Edwards, publisher, of the Daily Journal/Daily Messenger of Seneca, South Carolina, where some of these pieces have appeared.

I deeply appreciate Charlotte Holt, of SCETV Radio, who has graciously allowed me to record some of these pieces for the radio show, 'Your Day.'

Finally, thanks to Lisa Hoffman, editor of Emergency Medicine News, where some of the pieces have also been printed.

I'm very grateful to all of the readers who have encouraged me over the years, and who have watched my children grow up, so far, with me. When you tell me that you feel as if you know my kids, then I feel as if my children have an extended family in many places. What a great gift you give to us!

And thanks to God for everyone listed, for all the things in life to write about and for all the teachers who taught me to love words.

This book was published by Booklocker, on the web at booklocker.com, a wonderful company that has made my first forays into publishing delightful and hopeful. To Angela and Richard Hoy, thanks a bunch. You're the best in the business.

Cover art by my friend Ray Keys, at www.theweeklys.com.

Preface

Because this book is about a family, my wife and I have tried to lay it out in a sort of loose chronological order. All of the pieces here can stand alone, but if read from start to finish, will show the gradual progression of a family. It is not meant to be a biography, but rather a series of snapshots of the wonder of life in a family; a series of insights into the things that give us real meaning and purpose, real joy and delight.

Any typographical errors can be attributed to the chronic exhaustion of parenthood. That may not be the reason for the error, but I'd like you to attribute it to something other than my carelessness, and the 'tired parent' excuse is as good as any. If that doesn't work, I'll fall back on the old stand-by, the 'tired doctor'. It's overused, but comes in handy for avoiding unwanted social obligations and explaining silly mistakes.

Table of Contents

The Serious Introduction xv
The Funny Introduction xvii
Impressionists 1
Eric Douglas 3
Children's Greatest Supporters 5
Freedom, Peace and Equality 10
Hold The Line 13
Housewives 16
Deer Hunter 19
Wendy Dog 22
The Lure Of The Curve 25
Beauty 30
Promiscuous Reader 34
Be Thankful For Things That Are Not 38
Imagine and Play 40
Currents 42
Boys Will Be Boys 45
I am not an animal! I'm a parent… 50
Altar Call 53
Last Call for Babies 57
Parent Gift 60
Hope 63
Dog-shui 67
Father Duty 70
Christmas Photos 73
Bathroom Break 75
Halloween 78
The Screaming Hornets 81
Nature Love 84
Pulling The Wagon 87
Cloning Cats 90

Rescue Heroes 93
The Museum of Memory 96
Breath Shepherd 99
Dryer Guy 102
Betrothal 105
Building 107
Leaving Home (for good) 110
Bookstores 113
The New House 116
Cupid 120
Human Voice 123
Bloody and Daisy 126
I Knew Charlie Brown 129
Cats Don't Hike 132
Farmer Ed 135
Gerbil Farm 138
Memories In The Heart 141
Kelly's Wedding 147
Puppy Obit 150
Shopping for Gifts 153
Leap Year 156
And I Pray 159
Archeology 162
Beach Exodus 165
Morality 168
What Were You Thinking? 171
Elijah Shifts Gears 174
The Between Time 178
Dance to be Alive 181
Magic of Women 184
Silence is a Commodity 187
Teaching Laughter 190
Alone with Dora 193

Christmas Can't Be Rushed...................................... 196
Oktoberfest 198
Blind Man's Child 201
Home Defense 204
Family Kingdom... 207
Love Your Wife... 240
Author Biography 243

The Serious Introduction

This book is a record of the things I love the most. It is, on its surface, a collection of columns I have written over the years about my wife and children, and about the joys and lessons of growing up with them. But, in its depth, it is an archive.

Every day of my life with them, I have watched beautiful things happen, laughed at funny ones, and been touched by the way time slips past us far too quickly. I have tried to take in everything that we have done or experienced together, tried to hold the moments and caress the delights. I have tried, with all the mortal effort I could muster, to dig my heals into this life and slow down time.

On many occasions, I have wished that I had taken photographs I did not take; wished that I had a tape recorder in my pocket to record every subtlety of voice and laughter, every poignant insight of my children, every happy sigh of their lovely mother.

But, life is what it is, and only a bit its wonder gets preserved; and as we know so little of our ancestors, it is clear that what we preserve only lasts a while in the memories of our loved ones.

So, this book is my gift to my family and to myself. It is a way to archive my absolute joy at being a husband and father, and to pass it down the years to my children, and theirs, and theirs. It is my thank-you note to Jan, to Sam, Seth, Elijah and Elysabeth. My way of giving back to them bits of their childhoods, and telling them in print what I tell them all the time with my words and (hopefully) with my actions: you are all amazing, and you give me the greatest joy this life can ever give a mortal man; I love you all with all my heart. I see this book as a way that, in addition to pictures and video, they can be reminded of the grand times we have had together, and God willing will continue to have for many years.

I will not know all of my descendents in this life. But what I want to say to them with this book is, 'if I were with you, I would tell you all the things this book does. And if I knew you, we would have such fun together. And down the years, from this life or from the next, I love you too.'

This book is also a way to see that other people, family near and far, friends past and present, and strangers distant in place and time will know what a gift God gave me in my life. And a way to say to them that what is most important on earth and in Heaven is the love, the joy, the laughter, the wonder that lies all about you, placed by heaven's grace right in your very lap.

Finally, this is a letter to men everywhere that your greatest adventure is the care and protection of your families. Be the man they need you to be, and you'll never be sorry, never be bored and never feel irrelevant.

So, I hope you enjoy it. I have enjoyed writing it. But more than that, I have enjoyed living it thus far. I pray, and hope that you will pray for us, that there will be many more editions and additions as the years roll on.

The Funny Introduction

Here is my life with my wife and children. It has been a life of constant discovery. You will find many of the lessons of my life archived here. There are lessons about the cataclysmic destructive power of children, the functional worthlessness of pets, the brilliance and apparent witchcraft wielded by wives, and the way that I, as a man, have virtually no skill at building or repairing anything. There are some serious lessons, but they are introduced in the preceding 'serious introduction'.

There are, contained in the pages of this little volume, lessons about the outdoors, the indoors, houses, jobs, food, cats and all the rest. Lessons about what to expect on extended vacations with four children in one vehicle, lessons on how to survive spending hours in public restrooms, and others on the inherent dangers of the places we call home. They may not be applicable lessons for you. That is fine. Hopefully, they will be funny lessons at the very least.

This book is divided into small, digestible sections. It is meant to be read in the bathroom, on the treadmill, at lunch, at bedtime, in the tree-stand, by the pool, while waiting in the veterinarian's office while something is removed from the dog, while waiting in the pediatricians' office while something is removed from the child. It is meant to be read behind your boss's back while slacking off of boring projects. It is meant to be read by husbands, as a way to prove their sensitivity to their wives. It is meant to be read by wives so that they can say, 'See! It happens to other families too!' It is meant to make you think and laugh.

As a physician, however, I have to make certain disclaimers. This book is not meant to be read while driving a vehicle or operating heavy or dangerous equipment. It is inappropriate to read it while operating a chainsaw, a firearm, a chipper-shredder or while trying to start a fire with gasoline. Don't do that at all, please. It will be fine to read this book while under the influence of pain medication. It may be funnier, and you may feel a need to buy more copies, buy more copies, buy many more copies.

If you have time on your hands, are not doing anything dangerous or illegal, and want to read it all at one sitting, that's great. But if you are a parent or spouse, you probably don't have that kind of luxury.

I hope that you have fun reading about our lives. Because ultimately, the stories are yours as well, set in a different house, town, state or country. By the way, we're tired of watching your dogs. Please come and get them.

Impressionists

My wife and I recently took our children to Atlanta to see the Impressionists exhibit at the High Museum of Art. We always enjoy our visits there and hope that the boys will learn to love art by degrees, although they are both very young. Sam, age four, looked quite the adult art lover as he walked about, tour cassette player over his shoulder, ear phones firmly in place. He seems to see art in the only way that a four year old can; through eyes of innocence. We strolled from painting to painting, amid the press of the crowd, trying to learn as much as we could in the short time available. Each painting had so much to say and so much to give. I don't know how much Sam absorbed. But even exposure can be an education so I think his experience was worthwhile.

His two-year old brother Seth, on the other hand, was ready to leave as soon as we arrived. He wanted to walk, then be carried. He wanted my earphones, then no earphones. He begged me to take him to see "Doug's First Movie." He held my head in his little hands, turned my face to his pleading eyes and said "Go outside, Papa, please!" One can only endure this sort of begging from a toddler for so long. Kissing his mother and brother goodbye for a while, we escaped into the April sunshine, where he was instantly in his element.

We went to the large grassy area adjacent the back of the museum. The day was warm with a pleasant wind and we chased one another around in circles until I thought we would collapse. We rolled on the ground and we wrestled and tickled as he shook with the laughter that God created especially for two year olds. I noticed that passersby, leaving the museum, looked at us and smiled.

One idyllic moment I was on my back in the new grass, holding him above me, his arms spread wide, his dimples deep, cheeks rosy, all smiles, blonde hair blowing in the breeze as blue eyes spilled bliss like fountains. I felt that sensation one has when time stops. It never stops for long enough, although that is something of an oxymoron. Maybe it stops forever when we glimpse something so perfect. I held him close and kissed him. I suddenly understood art.

As I learned from the exhibit, Impressionism was an attempt to represent a moment in time, often a moment of daily life. Why would an artist do this? Why make a picture of something so mundane as a garden or someone bathing? To preserve the beauty of the moment is what we want every day of our lives, whether we are painters or not. We want to take our fleeting glimpses of eternal truth and beauty and preserve them in this temporal plane. We know, in our hearts, that all things will pass away. The paintings of the great masters will go to dust or ashes as surely as we. The sculpture of Michelangelo will crumble to the earth from which it was born. The music of Mozart will one day be played for a last time, then be lost in antiquity. And if not lost to history, each will be lost to every one of us as we pass from this world.

But all of those artistic media are ways to take what really matters and keep it, so that we can see it over and over, and so that others may in some small way glimpse through the pinhole we held up to infinity so briefly and see a transient image of the things that are timeless. Things like love, joy, sadness, wonder and their glorious connections.

Although I am a physician, not an artist, I wish that I could have painted my moments with Seth. I wish that I could have painted them in some magical way that would combine his voice, his look, his feel and smell with our intense love for one another. Then I would frame it with the sun and breeze that we basked in.

I think that was what the Impressionists wanted as well. Because that, dear friends, is art.

Eric Douglas

Some dear friends of ours just brought home their newly adopted son. He is the product of a long emotional (and physical) journey that involved many false starts, detours and sudden stops. I'm certain that the process was more difficult than any 40-week pregnancy and I would have understood if they had stopped trying, just to avoid the pain. Fortunately, their love of a child they had never met pulled them forward through the trials and now they are head over heals for a little boy that now has them completely in his grasp. This boy has no idea, as he eats and sleeps his time away, that he has fallen into a gold mine of absolute devotion.

I'm looking forward to watching our friends as they grow into the skin of parenting. It always feels a little funny at first; sometimes too tight, sometimes too loose. Then, with remarkable ease, it stretches or shrinks to who we are and suddenly parenting fits. Having spoken to them, I believe that the transition is occurring with ease. But there's another process I want to follow that will take longer to observe. I want to watch the process by which their little one becomes like them.

But how much will he be like them? They don't share any genetic bonds, after all. In an age of biotechnology, it seems all too easy to make the point that genetics are everything. And to some extent, it's true. Our bodies are complex mosaics of millions of genetic determinants. Everything from the color of our hair to the length of our lives is determined, in large and small ways, by the genes passed to us from our parents, and their parents and countless ancestors. Some of our diseases are hidden like land mines in the chromosomes that contain our blueprints. And so are many of our strengths and glories. The human genome is far from completely understood, but we may find that our temperaments, our talents, even our tastes are written in the chemical code of our cells. Modern science seems ready to settle the argument of nature versus nurture without much struggle.

However, the final verdict isn't in yet. And that's why I'm excited to observe our friends and their adopted child. In this unscientific study of one family, I expect to see how a child becomes like his parents without the benefit of all-powerful DNA.

It has begun already, of course. From the time his infant eyes opened on the cloudy world above him, he has seen the smiling faces and teary eyes of two people who transmit themselves to him in their expressions and voices. And when they held him for the first time, he learned a little of the strength of his mother and gentility of his father. These traits, modeled for him, are becoming his own.

As the months and years pass, he will have his parents' laughter and tone of voice. I expect his mind to be full of the things that drive them: love of learning and hard work, a sense of wonder and beauty and antiquity, and a burning passion for truth. He will have a body molded by activities that his mother and father teach him to enjoy and by habits which they teach him to practice. Every day of his life, in fact, his mother and father will sculpt him in their own image until he becomes their heir in every way, bursting beyond the narrow confines of our understanding of inheritance.

One day, when this little boy is a man, I feel confident that he'll walk into a room where I am and I'll look and think how remarkable it is that he is just like the parents who raised him. I'll watch him move and hear his voice and the content of his thoughts, and know that he became like those parents without chromosomes, genes or DNA. When that happens, I'll know I was right: that who we are is determined not so much by the bodies our parents pass to us, as by the sure, certain and infinite force of love.

Children's Greatest Supporters

Standing before me several weeks ago was an excited four-year-old boy with a new red backpack and a goofy smile. He was starting his first day of kindergarten and next to him was his two-year old brother wearing a blue backpack, oblivious to the fact that he was only coming along for the ride.

We took pictures and loaded the children into the car for the trip down Highway 28 to Bountyland Baptist Church where Oconee Christian Academy is located. It is a wonderful place filled with teachers and administrators dedicated to the education and welfare of its students from preschool through senior year. I knew that this was a good place for my child to learn.

But even as I was pleased with his courage, even as I was satisfied that he would be taught well and treated kindly, I secretly hoped that Sam would bail out. After all, I felt a little guilt even sending him at his age, knowing that he would spend so many of his future days in classrooms. My mind raced with reasons that he should not go to school since K-4 is elective, serving more for Sam's enjoyment than anything else. I found it especially stressful to send him. Irrational fears and worries are hard for me to avoid when it comes to my boys and my list is not short.

But more than fear, I wondered if the adults at his school would appreciate him. I wondered if his teachers would see him as the amazing creation that he is. Would they see the magnificent mind that he has or appreciate the complexity of his visions? I wondered if they would understand that he is a preschool mystic, who says his eyes are spirits, talks to the moon and tells me that God will give me good dreams. Would they recognize fear on his cherubic face? Then I realized that I wasn't being fair.

The thing is, we all want our children's teachers to think that our offspring are the greatest, smartest, strongest and most beautiful children ever born. To each of us, in very real ways, they are. Thus every teacher starts the school year with an unbearable burden. That burden is to love each student as a parent would.

Sam's teachers will doubtless grow to love all of their charges. But when I ask myself if they will love him as I do the answer must be no. Only parents can give a child the love that sees them as most perfect in the universe. This love isn't some irrational fantasy. It is the natural order of things. We are made to love our own children supremely. We are destined to be fiercely partisan toward them. This helps insure their survival. This contributes to their happiness and ours, for the present and future well being of our children is the true joy of devoted parents.

However, parents have often abdicated that place which we should have defended most ferociously of all. We are meant to be their champions from the moment they come to be. We are to defend and protect them, we are to embrace and accept them and see them as the embodiment of all that is beautiful and good. But as a nation we have erroneously placed schools and teachers in this hallowed place in the hope that they will give each child the total devotion that is only possible from us.

This is grossly unjust, leading to disappointed parents and frustrated educators. It makes parents criticize the educational system more harshly because we expect from it something that is not able to give. And it makes good teachers feel like failures when their best attempts to nurture do not meet the needs of students or the hopes of parents. Even while teachers love mightily, they cannot and should not be parents in the development of students' worth and integrity. The ultimate influence upon children's lives is love, richly lavished upon them at home. This love, this best earthly metaphor for the love of God, is our responsibility and privilege as parents alone.

Sushi

An addiction is a terrible thing. It creeps up on you. One day, you're fine. There isn't anything you need. Then suddenly, out of the blue, the monkey jumps on your back. You find yourself doing anything it takes to get a fix. You feel elated when you get what you want. You feel dejected when you can't have it. My dog Max understands this. He has cat food issues. In spite of the way that we have strategically placed the Meow Mix behind a gate, and regardless of his bowl full of dog chow, Max wedges his body into the slats, reaches with his paw and eats dry tuna and egg cat food like his life depended on it. I've heard him in the night, whining and moaning because the cat food was out of reach. He really has a problem. Anyone know a dog addictions counselor?

But I'm not going to talk any more about Max. I'm going to talk about me. A doctor. A professional with control over his faculties: a father of four: husband of only one wife: and tragically, shamefully addicted to sushi.

It's like a lot of addictions. You hear about it and laugh. "I'd never want that! Raw fish? No way." But then, a friend says, "just try a little, I'm buying." You start slow. A simple California Roll. After all, what's the harm? Rice, seaweed, cooked crab- meat, avocado. No one has a problem with that, right? Before long, you're looking at the menu a little more seriously. You think, "raw spicy tuna, that's exciting!" And sure enough, you pop it in your mouth with some wasabi and soy sauce and it's off to reefer madness.

Next, it may be fish eggs, or something with octopus. It may be my personal favorite, Unage, which is eel. (The things I'd do for a hit of eel right now). And then, the unique flavor isn't enough. You start to need more quantity. At first six pieces of salmon were fine. Suddenly you need more. I'm up to three rolls now. That's 18 pieces of sushi. I can't help it. It's not that I need it; it's just that I want it. I can quit anytime. Really.

I've also branched out into sashimi. Sashimi is a raw piece of fish with no rice or vegetables to adulterate it or diminish the taste. It's pure delight. Sashimi, to a guy like me, is almost a religious experience. My wife says my eyes roll back. I'm transported to another dimension. I don't think I've ever seen heaven, but I think that I once saw Tokyo in my state of rapture. Jan likes sushi but doesn't have the same sort of addictive issues I have. Fortunately, she's the responsible one and always comes along to drive in case I'm too full to concentrate on the road after eating.

I've tried sushi all across the Upstate of South Carolina, and everywhere else I can try it. My favorite place to go locally is Uptown Sushi Bar and Café in Clemson. They're like family. The pusher next door who understands what you need, where you come from. Sadly, my little problem began after my trip to Japan last summer. If I had been in the throes of this problem back then, they might still be searching the back street sushi houses of various cities for my pathetic body, washing dishes for one more hit.

I guess it could be worse. I could be terminally addicted to chocolate. Migraines saved me from that one. If not, it would be "paging doctor jowls!" I could be a pastry junky, offering work excuses and my monthly salary in exchange for chocolate filled croissants. In the big picture, I guess sushi isn't so bad.

But I need to be vigilant for other chinks in the armor. Just the other day my wife gave me a bite of her Butterfinger McFlurry from MacDonalds. My eyes rolled back. "What's in this thing, crack? I want one!" She drove away from the drive-through as fast as she could.

I didn't really need one, you know. I just liked the taste.

Freedom, Peace and Equality

The sun is low on the horizon. It is muggy but the faintest breeze blows across Sertoma Field in Walhalla, South Carolina. The spring grass is thick and green. The parking lot and creek bank by the road are filled with cars and trucks as young men and women in baseball, softball and T-ball uniforms cross the bridges. Families unpack folding chairs and coolers, staking out claims on patches of grass or bleachers.

There is a sense of community; a sense of all things American that pervades the place. Bankers sit alongside construction workers; stay-at-home moms sit by those who sell real estate. Insurance agents and engineers coach the kids. It is the sweet smell of democracy, the essence of who we are. No one is more important or less and everyone cheers for everyone else.

I'm there for my 5-year-old son's T-ball game. It is a sport worth watching, combining as it does elements of baseball, bird-watching, flower-picking and sandcastle building. In addition to cheering my son on, I get to do something else I enjoy. I get to watch the crowd. And watching I can see that T-ball, Little League Baseball and softball all are beautiful metaphors for what our country is.

We may celebrate Memorial Day with remembrances of battles and heroes. But what we were meant to have, what those who fought desired for us is exactly what transpires on spring nights on that field in the middle of Oconee County, SC. Because they wanted us to live free, at peace and with equality. And that is what I see when I look around at all the different games on all the different fields on those several acres of peace.

Freedom is there in abundance. It pervades the place. Attendance is mandated only by love of family and limited only by the constraints of job or personal responsibilities. No federal identification to be inspected as families make their way to the games. No political officer to suggest how they should spend their time.

Peace is there as well. Some parts of America are not so peaceful, where crime disrupts what could be lives of serenity. But there, in that little valley, peace suffuses all. No fear of warfare makes parents look skyward for bombers. No artillery thumps in the distance as fearful children try to make the most of a few moments of play. The field is not strewn with mines or grenades. No troops patrol with automatic weapons, rounds chambered and ready to fire. And there is equality. Not the equality of postmodern political engineering. Not the guarantee that everyone will always have the same things or the same money or the same position. This equality is more powerful.

It is an equality that says that all men and women are of the same fundamental value. That they have a place of worth not defined by the externals that many would like to equalize. That each persons' worth is divine and immutable, rather than transitory and that equality allows them all a chance at –- not a promise of -- the same success.

The children playing exhibit this equality of opportunity for they have the chance to be many things. Fighter pilots and grade school teachers will come from the young athletes on the field, as will surgeons and salesmen, lawyers and contractors. In America, as in their games, they are all equally valuable.

The reason that our ancestors and loved ones sacrificed themselves was to give us a chance to experience common joys in an uncommon land. Certainly, they suffered and died for noble beliefs: for the success of an experiment in government that has yet to be matched in the history of mankind; for the freedoms that are so fundamental to us, like speech, religion, personal defense and many others. But surely those who are gone, as well as those who remain, would admit that they suffered to preserve the mundane as well as the lofty. And that their blood was spilled, their bodies broken for ball games on spring evenings as surely as they were for the high ideals inscribed on the stone facades of Washington's buildings.

Hold The Line

The greens have been hung at College Street Baptist in Walhalla where my family and I attend church. Last Sunday morning we observed the second Sunday in Advent. The service included carols, candles and scripture; just what my wife and I love this time of year.

But in the midst of the beauty of the service with its deep seasonal message, we shot quick, desperate glances at one another over two rambunctious children, who alternately climbed, crawled, wrestled, cried and screamed through the service. I thought our pastor should have closed the service with the prayer, "Lord, please keep the Leap children safe from parental peril".

It was a long day, as each offspring vied for the most attention, coming up neck and neck in inspiring us to anger. My wife Jan holds to the single hope that this is, as she calls it, the "season of blackmail", when we can remind our four year old that Santa is watching. I'm sure it's a pagan, duplicitous way to parent, but we're just trying to hold the line.

But then it occurs to me that many people are trying to do just that. Just hold the line. We think that we can all achieve great things in the holiday season. We want to be generous givers of charity, tireless employees and useful members of our community. We all hope to be loving and patient parents who never raise tired voices at the cherubic faces for which we prayed so long. But the truth is life is more of a battle than a Norman Rockwell print.

Christmas reminds us of this every time it comes around. The shopping overwhelms with cost and crowd. The needs of the needy seem more poignant as we gather around our own lush trees, under which lie a king's ransom in gifts that most of the recipients don't need. And then there is the spirituality. We struggle to fit it in. I struggle to grasp it. The birth of Christ is only the commencement of the mystery, enigmatic as swirling stars, simple as a stable. And there it is again, an oppressive list of things we cannot begin to do or grasp in this single harried span of 31 light trimmed days.

It isn't actually the inability to do all we hope. The problem lies in the guilt that accompanies that perceived failure to perform. If only I could play with my boys enough or help their mother more, as she is due to deliver our third in May. If only I could offer her more rest and romance, study more medicine, visit my family so many miles away. Yet the end of the day rolls around and she and I lie exhausted by sleeping children and recognize that, once again, we only held the line.

But, that's enough. Ask a veteran of combat if they felt guilt when they kept their lines from being broken. If, at the end of the days fighting, they believed they were failures for having succeeding only in not retreating, not dying. They will doubtless say that they were just glad to be alive. My life bears no analogy to combat, but am I glad to be alive. Every day that I don't lose my temper is a small victory. Every day that I breathe and my family has health, food, shelter and clothing is a day that I have not lost. Never mind the innumerable blessings of friendship, career, respect, freedom, hope and a million other constellations in my personal universe.

I know that many people are struggling. In fact, my worries and concerns are laughable compared to the cosmic battles that many endure. Imagine the pain of war, genocide, bone-breaking poverty and terminal disease. Try to picture Christmas as a refugee on muddy, mine-strewn roads in the icy Balkan winter. Simply consider being a single parent on minimum wage, whose children scarcely stay warm; children for whom a coat is more desirable than a toy.

Christmas has many meanings. But if it has one at all, it is that Christ came to the broken, as the broken. Poor as dirt, born to an unwed mother in a nowhere town, in a defeated, occupied nation at the end of a millennium. He came to offer hope to everyone who just couldn't seem to win; and to help hold the line, while they wait for victory.

Housewives

My boys are sound asleep as I write. They have played with great energy today; a sort of parasitic energy that accumulates even as it drains from their parents. My wife Jan went to Greenville tonight, to have dinner with friends at one of our favorite restaurants. The times when she is away are good for us. They give her a much-needed break from full time mothering. They give me an immense renewed respect for what she does. Because I believe she has one of the hardest jobs on earth.

I often see female patients who, when asked what their job is, reply "I don't work, I'm just a mother and housewife". This does not represent their lives very well, for that combination is certainly among the most arduous and least appreciated of all career options. There are seldom booths on high school career day that celebrate the life of the full time mother and housewife. It is underrepresented in modern literature and film, somehow being seen, I fear, as an enslavement rather than a conscious choice. But I believe that a great many women do, in fact, choose this path because they see beyond its popular banality to its high nobility.

There is much about this path that is mind-numbing and monotonous. Jan often speaks of her longing for conversations with adults. I don't think I qualify, especially when I run through the house playing Batman and Robin with the boys. She spends hours doing laundry and cleaning. She shaves years from her life trying to mold our sons into reasonable human beings not bent on thievery or murder (skills which almost all children possess in rudimentary form from birth). She loses weeks of sleep when they are sick at night and climb onto our bed in the wee hours for water, milk or simply comfort. And she is carrying our third child now, a task I do not envy. Even my recent kidney stone cannot compare, for it's discomfort was less than a day of my life, whereas she is only in her seventh month of the nausea, pain and irreparable physical changes that accompany baby making.

But despite all the discomfort, lost sleep, screaming babies and cluttered playrooms, I know she wouldn't trade jobs with anyone. She knows that her job is honorable beyond measure. I give her credit for the comfort of our home, the well-being of our children, the very richness of our lives. I thank her for the fact that my two and four-year-old boys say thank you, please and sorry, and that they are constantly in a state of laughter and smiles. It is she who ensures that they say grace at meals and that they love to learn. It is she who gives me the support I need to support my family.

This sounds as if I abdicate my duties to her, the typical health professional who lives for work. In fact, I am home quite a lot. I take my responsibilities to her and the children very seriously. But, she is the anchor. She is the constant, while I may come and go depending on work schedules. She is the cornerstone of our family; a critical role in a world is in which the only permanence is impermanence.

Occasionally, after a day of feeding, dressing, playing, wrestling, disciplining, bathing, and reading to the boys, we comment on how hard it would be to live life as a single working parent. I feel a wave of fear and my heart goes out to those who are. We are thankful we can be a team. But she is, now as always, the most valuable player.

As an emergency physician, I have what many would consider a difficult job. Every minute that I work may be punctuated by some disaster. I care for any and every illness and every variety of person, at all hours of the day and night. But, compared to the genuine, full-time, stay-at-home, 24-hour a day mom and wife, my job seems like selling hot dogs at the ball-park. So to all those women who are "just moms and housewives", my hat is off. Remind me to write you a work excuse to give to your husbands. You need some time off.

Deer Hunter

I may be one of the worst whitetail deer hunters in South Carolina. I'm convinced that my schedule is faxed to 'deer central' so that every potential day off that I could hunt is known far in advance by my worthy quarry. I have only started deer hunting since living in South Carolina but thus far I have done most everything I think I should do, including using tree stands, scent covers, doe urine, grunt calls and antler rattling. I am a washout. But I will keep trying. I'll keep taking my chances that each day afield may only result in another long episode of sitting outside, watching the wind blow and seeing little else but flying leaves and the occasional extremely loud gray squirrel. The hunt is more than the kill and I am coming to appreciate that.

Don't get me wrong, that isn't just rationalization. When I killed two caribou in Alaska last August, I enjoyed the success. I enjoyed every minute of work that it entailed, both before and after the shots. But it becomes plain that sitting quietly in the fields or forest is much more powerful a thing than just the success of bringing home the game. It is an exercise in developing many internal characteristics, as well as physical skills. And it is, in truth, a matter of the heart.

Today the December sky is drizzling a cold rain and I am scheduled to work. I had hoped to try again today but having to work at 11pm after sitting in the cold rain has left me with less zest for the hunt than I would ordinarily have. The longest deer season in the United States is drawing to a close and unless something changes this week, I will have a dry year.

But the hunt does things that we do not count on. It brings us in touch with a past we seldom feel in a computerized, fast food age when all we want or need seems to appear magically. It teaches us; first, that food comes from somewhere. That if one eats meat, someone has killed. Period. Steaks do not grow on stems. But this is only the beginning. It teaches us the qualities of planning and foresight. What does the weather look like? Will a cold front leave me shivering in Sumter National Forest, when I am wearing light summer clothes? Will there be deer where I hunt? Will I have a tree to put my stand into? Will I be there alone or will I have to be careful not to intrude on other hunters?

Still, there is more. The hunt teaches us the twin graces of stillness and silence. We move and move so much. Our lives are in non-stop motion. How difficult to learn how not to move. To sit and have economy of movement, such that even scratching one's nose becomes a choreography that takes short paths and slow contraction of stiff muscles. Silence itself is so unusual. There are automobiles and aircraft, televisions and stereos; there is beeping and banging and the loud stomp of our feet on concrete, or in our homes. People seek vacations in silence, so precious a thing it is. But the hunter does not need to go far. He needs only to find his favorite spot, in the still of morning or evening, with a few necessary items and a love of quiet.

In these skills, in these efforts of preparation, stillness, silence, this faint but ever present risk of venturing away from civilization, perhaps the greatest gift comes. There comes the gift of self-examination. In the brush of leaves in the autumn wind, while listening intently to the mosaic of sounds considered perfect stillness by most persons, we have the chance to hear what so few do. The sounds of our own hearts, the poetry of our thoughts and the pounding, incessant, of the things we love. I have found myself frequently more in love with life, family, country, God while hunting than I ever could while sitting in the bright lights of an office, the press of traffic or madness of a mall.

Little surprise that the last day I was out on my property in Tamassee, South Carolina, I saw a man a quarter mile away, standing on a hilltop. Tempted to remind him that it was private property, I watched him from cover, walking around the knoll. I elected to drive around to where he was as I left for home. When my car passed his location, I saw him from behind, standing in the wind on the hilltop, arms spread out in the sunshine in what could only be called an act of joyful worship. I left quietly. I didn't kill anything that day. But I bagged some wisdom as I saw a man loving the world as I do. And that was enough.

Wendy Dog

Do you think dogs go to heaven? I've never been really convinced myself. I always felt that animal life ended when it ended. However, my opinion changed when we had a little tragedy a while back. One of our dogs, Wendy, went unusually far from home and was killed by a car. My wife found her as she drove the children to school. Wendy, less than one year old, came from the pound for Seth's third birthday. She was energetic and gentle. In spite of the fact that she managed to chew up everything she came into contact with, from paper cups to pieces of metal, we enjoyed her. She was, among the four dogs living here, the "life of the party".

Seth was appropriately devastated. Although I wasn't present when Jan told him the news, she reports that he cried and cried. Since that day, he hasn't shed a tear. But he has been very curious about Wendy's fate. We explained to Seth that Wendy is in Heaven. We didn't really make the distinction of dog heaven versus people Heaven. That's too much theology for a three-year-old.

Having accepted this fact, Seth continually asks when he can go to see his dog in Heaven. He asked me one night if we could "ask God to bring Wendy back down". He misses his dog. But, in his young mind, there isn't any doubt that his dog lives on and that he will be re-united with her one day.

Now this may be because we told him so. But I think it goes further. I think it is because we are programmed for forever. Death is a difficult concept for us because, quite frankly, it isn't supposed to happen; and deep in our primordial souls, we know it.

From the time we are small, we know wonder. We sense it all around us in nature and if we are lucky in the love bestowed upon us. In this acceptance of wonder is the seed of eternity. Because somehow, I believe, we are designed to feel that life is too wondrous for a few short years. I am convinced that it is in our hearts from birth. And I am equally convinced that this is the reason that even my three-year-old has no problem with the concept of heaven, the belief in perpetuity.

Eternity is a concept central to most major religions. It may take the form of linear time culminating in eternal life or punishment, as in Judaism, Christianity and Islam. Or it may be that of multiple, repeating cycles of life and death, as in Hinduism and Buddhism. Whatever the faith, there is a sense that nothing good, especially human life, ever really goes away. And I like to believe that goes for dogs, too.

For many who do not share this belief, the concept of eternal life is nothing more than a cruel deception. Why waste time putting off for another life? Make the most of the life you have here! And I couldn't agree more. The problem is, when you make the most of this life, when you revel in it, when you love every minute and ache for more, when you love and lose, as I have seen so many times in my life and practice, you often find yourself believing that there can't really be an end. This is the problem facing Seth. Put simply, "My dog was good. I loved my dog. I miss my dog. I want to see my dog again. There must be another chance for me to do so."

If it works for dogs, it must work for humans. How can the love that we cultivate in life for so many people simply vanish with something so mundane as a last heartbeat? It's irrational. That this limited physical form should be the sole protector and vehicle for our hearts, which overflow with all the grandeur and beauty around us, well, it doesn't add up.

So I suspect that Wendy is in heaven. I also suspect we'll see her again. Grandma Leap had a saying. "When you get to heaven, you'll be surprised to see some folks. That's OK. They're just as surprised to see you!" I imagine Wendy, gnawing a heavenly bone, looking up at us one day coming through the gates and saying to herself, "Seth I expected, but those other humans? Imagine that!"

The Lure Of The Curve

A few weeks ago, Jan and I went with two of our friends to a local fondue restaurant. We have always loved eating there and our friends had never been there before. We wanted to share it with them, knowing as we did that they love a good meal as much as we. This became obvious when we had crab legs with our friends on another occasion and the lovely lady of the pair was noted to have a large piece of crab in her hair after a particularly zealous attack upon a steaming plate of crab legs.

The dinner was, as always, wonderful. The ambiance was so relaxing. The service was courteous and prompt. And last but not least, the food was outstanding. Now, we aren't food critics. We never look at the wine list, because we never learned to like it. Like good Southerners, even our finest meals are accompanied by sweet tea. But for simple folks like us, that dinner was grand.

It's part of a long tradition of ours. We've been "loving each other with food" since we met in college. Back then it was pizza and malted milk balls. Now we are grown, the food and the price -tag have changed, but the idea is the same. Food is one of our greatest joys. We seek it out. We revel in it. We've often wondered why we weren't big as houses. But somehow we've managed to enjoy food without abusing it.

The thing is, we rarely drink any alcohol, do not smoke, don't do drugs and really do not have any major vices. So we're left with food (and having children). It works out well, not only for us but also for local restaurateurs, several of whom have likely purchased major appliances thanks in no small part to our efforts.

But it's women and food that I really want to address. And the point I want to make is this: society has gotten a little ridiculous in its fascination with women who look like willow branches. I cannot imagine dating or marrying one of those women who order things like "a small house salad, no cheese, no croutons, light oil and a glass of water with a twist of lemon" as dinner entrees. I wouldn't be impressed. I'd be scared.

I'm not sure, but I think that it would cause me to question the passionate nature of such a creature. I mean, a woman who loves food is a woman of passion, a woman who understands how to enjoy life. I love my wife for many reasons. One of them is that, while being beautiful, she still likes to eat a good meal. She isn't ashamed to order steak and she isn't morally opposed to ordering lamb. She likes appetizers and loves bread. I like the same so our dinners, especially our dinners out, are momentous events in which we try our best not to leave anything untried and after which we can just make it to the car before we need to sit down again.

She is currently 24 weeks pregnant. Anyone who reads my column regularly will be asking 'when are you going to give that woman some peace?' The answer is soon, very soon.

But her pregnancies have given her a mother's curve that I love. Thus, we don't spend a lot of time worrying about our special dinners. Of course, we don't sit night after night before the television eating brownies and drinking soda either. We try to exercise regularly. But I feel that a curve is every woman's birthright. And any woman or man who denies it is just mean. Besides, a man who looks askance at his lover's curve is a lunatic who is missing out on another of life's great joys: a happy woman.

Learning to Love Learning

This time of year always take me back. It reminds me, every year, of what it was like to start college. Jan and I were having lunch in Clemson just the other day and the restaurant was filled with parents and students, some freshmen, some returning. I saw the angst in the parents' eyes. I saw the anticipation in those of their sons and daughters. I heard the nervous laughter that comes with such a significant event in life. Jan and I both recall the delicious uncertainty of education. We love the taste of new knowledge and the effort to perform, to accomplish, to read the minds of professors and give back what they want, all the while satisfying our own desire to learn. It is a rich memory, which grows more delightful every year that we move from it.

It occurred to me, however, that another kind of matriculation was occurring in our home. Sam, age 5, started kindergarten this year. Admittedly, it isn't the same as taking him to a new city and leaving him, but it is momentous. We are always jealous of anything that competes for our influence over the children; and school, whatever the grade, is one of those things. But I cannot begrudge him. He is entering a time of learning just as important as any Clemson freshmen. Now it is mandatory and he is starting the journey that will help take him to maturity and ultimately to the knowledge he will need to find his full potential, to support himself and contribute to society. A bit of a heavy burden to lay on a little guy, so I won't tell him all the ramifications just yet.

But whatever the age, wherever the school, I think that kindergarten and college have something in common. Or rather, that they should have something in common. For school to have any salutary effect on a student, that student must want to learn. Further, wanting isn't really enough. That student has to love knowledge. When that happens, learning is more than annoyance, tests, teachers and vacations. It is a journey into wonder.

Plenty of people go through life becoming functional, even wildly successful, without a love of knowledge. Because what they have is an efficient way to process information. The difference is subtle, but real. Information has utilitarian ring to it, while knowledge exists for its own sake. Knowledge is that thing which we want to know, even though it may give us no earthly gain. Even though it may damn us and reveal truths that shatter our myths about ourselves, or our world. Knowledge pulls its disciples forward through uncertainty into enlightenment.

As we shake our heads over education and each political party jockeys to say they'll fix everything educational, I can't help but wonder if it will matter. I interact with a lot of college and high school students and it saddens me to hear comments like "I hate to read!" Or, "I like my classes in my major, but I can't stand all of that English and History. It's useless!" Clearly, many of the persons who make these comments are bright and articulate. But somewhere along the line someone failed them by neglecting to instill in them a love of learning for its own sake.

Jan and I often wish we could go back to school. Not to study more of what we comprehend, but to somehow attain to a fraction of the galaxies of knowledge we do not understand. At some point in our past we became hungry for learning. The same feeling hits us as we enter a large bookstore or library. There is an immensity; a sense of how much we can never grasp in spite of our best efforts. It is as thrilling as it is somehow melancholy. One life seems all too short.

As each of our children enter school, we hope we can teach them to love learning. Because one thing is certain: all of the teachers and accountability, all of the testing, all of the new buildings, computers and money that we heap upon school systems are wasted if they are used on children who view knowledge as a necessary evil. The only hope for education is for our children to see all learning as a sacred, joyful act. And it falls most heavily upon families to instill this passion as early as possible, so that it can be a blessing for a lifetime.

Beauty

A 35-year-old physician meets a beautiful co-ed on a flight, far from his wife and children. They laugh, joke and share stories about their lives. Then...they go their separate ways. There are no lurid details. No touching except for a handshake. There is nothing to feel guilty about. Not the sort of story most men want to read. But the sort of story most men, at least married men, could find meaningful.

I'll call her Robyn. She was a delightful college student who was as erudite as she was lovely. Her hair was blonde and perfect, her nails were immaculate, her suit stylish and form fitting. She reduced every stereotype of dumb blondes to a pulp. She was on the way to the wedding of an old boyfriend. We talked for at least two hours on what would otherwise have been a painfully boring trip. For a traveling married man, it was a dream come true. I doubt if it was what beautiful, single women dream of, as I subjected her to pictures of my wife and children, as well as unnecessary details of the conference where I had just spoken.

During our layover at a connecting airport we talked. Then we shook hands and I wished her well. It was a wonderful encounter, without exchanges of phone numbers or e-mail addresses. But I hoped afterward that I hadn't misled her into thinking that married men are safe, because we aren't. We are tragically near-sighted about beauty and in our aesthetic myopia we are easily tempted to think that someone younger or more exciting would be a possible replacement for the wife of our youth.

The thing is, for all of Robyn's elegance and style she was probably not yet fully developed in her beauty. She was young and doubtless had experienced some of the trials and joys of love. But I doubt if she had been consumed and devoured by it. She had not surrendered to it wholly as one does when married. She had yet to put on the mantle of loveliness that only devotion and trial can produce.

I met my wife Jan and our then five-month-old son, Elijah, as I entered the airport at home after that flight. Jan wore an old blue dress that she describes as frumpy. I love it, for it is as comfortable as home to me. Elijah was hanging from her chest in a carrier that made him look like an errant paratrooper hung in a tree, awaiting rescue. She was tired, having had all three of our children for a week while I lectured. Her hair was mussed, she wore little makeup and her nails were, fortunately, still attached to her fingers. But for all that, she was more beautiful than ever, because her beauty is born of love.

For the past 16 years that we have known one another and the past 10 that we have been husband and wife, she has born the difficulties of relationship and parenting with a grace that can only come from absolute devotion. In so doing she has grown into a sculpture so refined, so flawless that she belongs on display as an inspiration to struggling wives and mothers all over the world. It seems that her trials have polished away the rough angles and exposed what she was meant to be. She was meant to be a mother, meant to be a wife who loves her husband unconditionally and to be herself, loved unconditionally. In becoming this, she has attained a beauty that far surpasses any young, untried woman that some married men might find the paragon of loveliness.

It seems apparent to me that love performs physical transformations that are beyond the scope of any plastic surgeon. Her hair is not made up each day in bows or curls. The children pull at it and she pushes it back in frustration. But it is beautiful to me because I have buried my face in it countless times to rest from my worries. Her hands are sometimes dry and usually her nails are short and unpolished. But they are perfect for they

31

provide every comfort for our three sons and myself. They feed us, they hold crying children and they hold my hand whenever I desire. Her eyes are tired, but they have looked upon me at my best and worst and continue to see me with love, even as they watch the children with a growing wonder and the vigilance of a lioness. Her figure has slightly rounded through the years, but it is the price of healthy children and it has curves that are known to me as well as I know my own body, perhaps better. When I hold her, I know that she isn't today's ideal fashion model. I don't want a model. I want the mother of my children, the love of my life, whom I have "loved with food" (as she put it) for many years.

That isn't to say young women can't have true beauty, for many young women have been through more than enough trials to mold them into true loveliness. But in general, it takes a few years and more than a few tearful arguments. It takes inconsiderate remarks and actions by husbands, sleepless nights and sick children. And it may take extra pounds, failed diets, disappointing birthdays and months with too little money for a real woman to come into the goddess-like state that I refer to and that my Jan has attained.

In the movie "Thomas Crowne Affair," Renee Russo's character said, "Men make women messy". Jan loved that line, because we do. Not only do we make our women messy with the struggles of living with us, but we change their bodies with children, we alter their dreams in favor of our own, we shake our heads as they age and cease to wear mini skirts and four-inch heals. All the while, of course, we ignore the harsh facts that we are turning gray or bald, that our belts are struggling to hold back years of good food, that our exercise isn't helping all that much and that young women don't think we're sexy after all.

I think I owe Robyn a debt of thanks. Not only did she keep me company on a dull flight, she reminded me of something critical. I don't want a college student, movie star or centerfold (anymore than they want me). I want my wife, just the way she is and just the way she's going to be. Beauty is a thing in constant evolution and transition. And as it moves from age to age in the women with whom we shared vows, we husbands need to remember that it may look a little different on the surface, but it is never more angelic and perfect than when we view it through eyes of love.

Promiscuous Reader

I am a promiscuous reader of books. Most readers would prefer the word "avid", or maybe the word "passionate". Some readers when defining their love of books, reduce it to "hobby" and include it on the list of favorite things that they write at Sunday School socials along with "Chinese food, travel and college football". But reading long ago left hobby for me. Now it is an affair. Or since I have said I am a promiscuous reader it is a series of affairs.

Let me say that I am a faithful husband to one wife. So the analogy does not represent all of my dealings in love. But knowing myself as I do, if I were not faithful, if I were not bound to my one wife by bonds of love and by my absolute belief in God, the Decalogue, my vows, my children and the bottom line stop gap of divorce attorneys, my love of books would resemble a love of women.

I cannot remain faithful to a book. When I go to the bookstore I wander the aisles and find one that catches my eye one that pulls me in. It may be the jacket, something in the art, something in the title, or even the font. It may be that superficial. The literary equivalent of wanting a woman because her hair is long, or blonde; or because it is red and pulled back into a loose ball on the back of her hair, so that wisps hang down along her neck while she reads through glasses that, on anyone else, would be ridiculous. I sometimes fall for a book that easily and so I buy it as I might approach a woman, because no foot ever looked so perfect in those heels.

Other times, of course, it is a set up. I have read about the book in the newspaper, or on-line. It was recommended to me by a friend. I have known the author's work before. I go to the aisles to meet the book as I might go to the café to meet the woman who is a friend of a friend, who was commended to me as "fascinating and honestly she really is beautiful and you have so much in common." And when I see her I know they were right at least at first. And when I want these books, I want them badly because they come with someone else to suggest them, someone else saying to me, "if you don't read this you'll regret it" as if they were saying, "you really should go out with her at least once."

Of course some books recommend themselves to me with more depth. I pause and read the back of the book or the inside flap. I get a sense of the story. I have a conversation with them with the characters and author, however brief. Like a chance encounter with some woman I would never have stopped to speak with but whose voice holds me just as the few paragraphs that outline her mind hold me. I need to know more. We must learn about one another. I must read the book.

And then there is the ultimate connection, when the combination so entrances that I know I will love the book. When the flap holds me, when I read a few paragraphs at random and the words seduce me by their arrangement, by their depth, by the way the story reaches inside me. And when it all fits, cover, title, font, flap, story, words, words, words. Hair, eyes, lips, body, dress, ankles, voice, ideas. When it all fits and she leans close to me and touches me casually. And without knowing more, I know that we are perfect and she was made, she was written for me.

Sadly, I am the modern man. Sometimes I am not at fault. The cover is a trick to conceal a terrible work like perfect makeup on the face of a shrew. Sometimes the recommendation, the fix-up, was just wrong. The matchmaker didn't know me, or her, well enough. The reviewer didn't know what I needed in the book he coaxed me to buy. We go out but part amicably because it just didn't work. I may even begin the book and fail to finish it. There just isn't enough to hold me.

But sometimes, more fully the modern man, I am simply promiscuous. And while half-way through my latest acquisition I am suddenly bored and as the words lie vulnerable before me, I leave and begin to read another. I am faithless and shameless. Even when I love a work, when I am touched and shaped by it, when I am full of its glory, recommending it to my friends, taking her to meet the family, I am going out at midnight searching for another. I am drawn, helplessly, into the next bookstore, stalking the aisles, touching and reading, sometimes even smelling the books for the love of them. Still reeling from my dark skinned, dark eyed brunette, who wears her hair in long curls, who wears blue-jeans with the elegance of an evening gown, I look around for the full, fair blonde, leaning against the checkout counter, décolletage before me.

I switch this way, book to book, genre to genre. Sometimes I try to elevate myself. I want literary fiction and so I find it. Highly vaunted, well-mannered, pedigreed. Its voice smooth and well trained. I love the way it lifts me, Appalachian hick, up to itself and the way its polished, turned phrases say things I have always thought but in ways I cannot fathom having written. But then, after a few cocktail parties, after a few more chapters, after a few days or weeks of feeling that I have over reached myself, I want less and I leave her screaming that I am nothing, do you hear me, nothing! And I find some story that speaks to me from the front porch swing, sundress blown in the faint, imperceptible breeze of Southern August. I find some story that speaks plainly to me with metaphors that match my education, a girl I can settle down with, a girl who laughs and makes love and has babies with no self consciousness, a book that makes its point without making itself the point.

But it doesn't matter. I'll be faithless to her as well. I leave her crying on the porch, I wander away looking, looking. Though I admit that the ones I love, truly love, stay with me. I visit them again from time to time again or the same authors whose sequels seem to me as appealing as an ex-lover's cousin. The ones I love haunt me and their words swirl in my head in memory of the heat of our time together; even the covers, the titles, the superficialities remembered like the small things about a woman, her nails, her perfume, the way she bit her lip when she was uncertain. But in the end, I am still a cad.

In the end, I will always be this way. An avowed literary bachelor, who cannot be still, cannot be trusted, cannot rise too far above himself. I'll always stalk the aisles for some new love, some new thrill, some new touch to reach inside to a place I didn't know existed.

I am a promiscuous reader.

Be Thankful For Things That Are Not

The last few nights Elijah, my 6-month-old son has kept his mother and me awake all night long. He is either nursing or crying so neither of us is sleeping. We are thus beginning to suffer the delusions and hallucinations that are the hallmark of the sleep-deprived.

Fortunately his 2- and 4-year-old brothers have slept a little better, albeit not by much. In short the Leap house is open all hours. At any time, on any given night you may find us awake rocking a baby while watching late-night TV or perhaps trying to soothe a toddler back into whatever dreams he was having before the dog barked and he awoke.

But a recent night was special. Somehow it seemed a little longer. We made the mistake of taking the children out too late and then going to bed late ourselves. If anyone doubts that humans can experience eternity let them listen to a baby crying from midnight to 6 a.m. But it is the reality of parenting. It isn't easy and it isn't always fun but it is worthwhile and deeply rewarding. It is also deeply moving as children teach us more than we ever knew we didn't know.

As we were preparing for bed I was holding Elijah while his mother was busy elsewhere in the house. He wanted to nurse, he was tired and he was as angry as a baby can be. He had gone from a simple cry to that soul-piercing wail that was designed to reduce adults to instant and total submission. I could not console him; I could not comfort him; I could offer him no relief from his mental and physical state. But I knew that nearby was what he needed. That Jan would soon rescue us both from our increasing annoyance with one another. Never were two males happier to see a woman than when she walked into the bedroom and took him from me.

38

But as he cried, as I tried my best to relieve his temporary anguish, I realized that somewhere in the world a parent was holding a hungry child and there was no relief in sight. There was no well-fed mother to nurse him; there was no formula to give him; there was perhaps, no clean water to stave off dehydration. That parent was probably hungry and thirsty as well and using every last reserve of energy to heroically give their child some remote chance of survival.

There has been a recent trend in the study of history to consider alternate history. That is to take events like World War II and change them and try to forecast how the world would have fared. What would have happened if Hitler had won? What would have happened if the Soviets first had the atomic bomb? These are of course academic questions with no solid answers, but they are an interesting exercise. And the same technique can be applied to one's life on an individual and very personal level.

Last night, for example, I was thankful that my children were not starving because for a few moments, I imagined that they were and marveled at my blessings. Sometimes I imagine that Jan or the boys are critically ill or have had an accident. (I don't do this one on purpose but because I am a habitual worrier). After having imagined this then seeing them come bouncing through the door to greet me – everything else seems to fall into proper perspective.

As Thanksgiving approaches, I am not suggesting that morbid thinking is an enjoyable hobby. I am only suggesting that it is just as important to be thankful for those things that are not, as for those that are. Maybe it's even a little more important. Because it is not only the presence of blessings that makes life excellent, but the absence of curses. And with a little thought I can make a long, long list of curses that are thankfully absent from my life.

Imagine and Play

Last night the children played their last soccer game of the season. They played well. It was a culmination of sorts, as every year they have played with more interest and delight. They have learned to run for the ball, rather than fear it. And they have discovered that the mass of other players that formerly interrupted their inspection of ant-hills and picking of flowers is in fact the place where the ball is located. I am proud.

But now that it's over, I doubt if they'll miss it. They see it as a pleasant distraction. It is a chance to play with friends, family and possibly an opportunity to eat pizza in a restaurant. But it is not a matter of great import. It is far less important to them than the delight of random un-directed play.

I watch them play and I am always fascinated. I frequently play with them and even as delightful as it is, I sometimes feel like an anthropologist investigating an unknown tribe, or studying a band of chimpanzees. Play is the natural state of the child. In fact, it is so natural in childhood that we have trouble following it as adults.

For example, my children will say to me, "We're lemurs! Will you be a lemur with us? You can be the ninja lemur! But not the normal one, you're the alien one with fire that shoots out of your fingers, OK? No, wait, we're your baby kangaroos that you caught in the woods. We escaped and you have to catch us with the blanket. That's your net. But we can fly and you can't. OK? But first, let's be rescue heroes playing hide and seek. And after that can we play with the castle? I'd like our knights to have a battle. Can we play chess?" You get the idea. Play is most thrilling to participate in and observe when it is random, uninhibited and propelled by the white-hot fire of imagination.

I have noted over the years that my children play less and less with the expensive toys that we buy and more and more with one another and with a few select and not too complicated toys that are their own preference. And I have also noted that when we drive them hardest with activities, they seem most to desire play. "Can we just stay home and play?" is a line I've heard many times. They enjoy traveling, but home with their things and their comforts' is where they ultimately want to be.

As a result of my studies of play, I've come to the conclusion that there are probably a host of children in America today who want nothing more than…less! In particular, they want less activities. They play some sports and take some lessons, because they desire to do so. But in many instances, they do it simply because they suppose that it's expected of them. They may even do it because they want to please parents who are excited about various activities themselves. But ultimately, they want simplicity.

They want food in their own kitchens and sleep in their own beds. They want the comfort of the familiar, the discipline of simple schedules that do not require palm pilots, day-timers or long range planning sessions. They want games that involve running around in the grass without rhyme or reason, following paths known only to them. They want to dance to the music we adults can't hear. They want to experience creation all around them with all five senses. They want insects, reptiles and amphibians. They want to wear pajamas and catch fireflies. They want a world that moves in small orbits, not large ones.

Activities serve a purpose. They hone athleticism or other skills. They teach citizenship. They introduce our young to the larger world. But equally important is the smaller world, in which they can feel safe and comfortable and in which they will grow strong, healthy, bright and creative simply by following the regimen encoded inside them since the beginning. Run, play, imagine, explore, eat and sleep. All the rest is too often too much.

Currents

The Chattooga River, not far from my home, is an incredible waterway. It has many faces and many uses. I have friends who hike miles to fish its waters for trout and other species. I have worked with many former raft guides who know the river like most of us know the road home.

Some sections of the Chattooga are glassy and calm and the swimming is easy. Section IV, where rafters and kayakers from all over the country come to play, is wild and untamed, dangerous and thrilling. It is a maelstrom of eddies and currents that thrill adventurers; it is also a death trap of underwater hazards and powerful hydraulics where some have perished.

But whatever section one sees or experiences, there is a force, a current that moves it forward. It is the unstoppable drive to go down to the sea. It isn't the same as the splashes and waves that break the surface, although they are part of it. Neither is it entirely represented by calm, which deceives us while tons of water pass by, subtly carving the river bed, slowly making jagged rocks smooth as millennia pass. It is more fundamental, more elemental. It is what rivers do. They cannot help but move forward. When they cease they are no longer rivers.

So it is with history, as we pass through times of chaos and issues, drama and emotion, wars, elections and revolutions. These things are merely breakers on the surface of the river of our existence. Our human lives and history seem so bound up in events. A quick tour of television history shows, a walk through the history section of the local library or book store, will reveal that the surface of our ancient waters is mostly recorded in waves and floods, rapids and waterfalls. And these are important for they are often the most visible of the events of time. They are quantifiable, though typically they represent the times when the river of history rises above its banks and does its most sudden and horrifying damage.

But what about the drive? What about the current that moves the river forward even without the turmoil of the surface? I found myself floating in it over the past week. It was a good thing. I have been beaten on the rocks for quite a while now as I have wrung my hands over crises and politics, economics and terrorism. Fortunately, I just got tired and drifted down into the depths of the river, where I discovered what I was missing.

I found it again playing with my boys in fallen autumn leaves with the evening air cool on our skin. I found it in their laughter and tears and in the humor of my 18-month-old who fell off the end of a slide and walked toward me with leaves and twigs sticking out of his mouth and nose. I found it when that same child sat on my lap in perfect stillness as I read to him and he began to make new words as his world opened ever further on knowledge and accomplishment. It was in the conversation of my five and three-year-olds, who every morning on the way to school tell me how God is sitting beside me and ponder issues of theology as only innocents can.

I found it powerfully in the movement of our unborn daughter within my wife, and in my wife's weary smile that says, "Is it time yet?" I saw it in the faces of other mothers and other children at Halloween parties and when the boys and I went out for trick or treat and the darkness and light combined in wonderful mystery.

What drives history? Too many things to recount. But it is driven most powerfully, for me at least, by love and wonder. Struggles and troubles come and go but good moves ever onward, however slowly, unstoppable. Humans will always suffer difficulties but beyond every dark descent is an ascent to recovery, into love of things that give the greatest peace, the greatest joy. The love of men and women, their love for their children, the knowledge and hope they instill in one another, the wonder of things holy, these are the currents, beneath all else, which propel us forward.

Boys Will Be Boys

I taught children's church this morning. In it were three little girls, Rebecca, Emily and Alyssa, with my youngest son, Elijah, tagging along. My two older boys bailed out on me in favor of sitting in the sanctuary with their mother. I think it was a function of a bag of candy and drawing paper but I could be wrong.

As I began to teach these three little princesses, I was stricken by what my friend Pat calls "the difference between an estrogen based system and a testosterone based system". He has one son and one daughter. I have three sons. But, come January, I'm going to have (gasp) a daughter.

Except for the fact that Rebecca and Emily routinely transmogrify into small animals (mostly cats and dogs), they were quintessential little girls. Alyssa, all in pink, spent almost the entire class trying to give Elijah his juice bottle. He looked like a lamb in a 4-H project. Oh, sure there was a little bit of destruction. But not boy destruction. That's only found on the Y-chromosome.

These days, boys get a lot of bad press. And as a health care professional and parent, all I can say is "phooey". Boys are just different. Somehow, in our primordial development as humans, we men were encoded with genes for, shall we say, destruction. As we grow and mature, we learn, with some notable exceptions, to mask these urges to demolish and maim. In little boys, these genes are frankly and proudly unmasked, such that destruction, accidental or intentional, is their daily "modus operendi."

Every day of our lives at home is an exercise in managing testosterone driven activity. It is a unique experience, requiring a subtle combination of emotional sensitivity, self-defense skills, the ability to repair or clean anything and a healthy knowledge of first aid. And that's just from 7 - 8 am.

Allow me to cite examples. One day I walked down our stairs to discover a toy super-hero (the Green Lantern, to be exact), lying at the bottom of the stairwell, a distance of some 15 feet. He had a child's blue glove over his head. The ordinary human, or perhaps parent of only a daughter, would ask, "Why would he have a glove on his head? It doesn't even match his costume! " The parent of boys asks, "What crime did Green Lantern commit to be subjected to ritual execution?"

Boys' minds just work that way. Say the word monster and you have a boy's interest. Say the word blood and you have his total attention. Offer a boy any benign household object that looks remotely like a weapon and he will turn it into one and then be your devoted servant. To further illustrate, we have friends who are devoted parents of two boys. These adults are artistic and soft-spoken. They are entirely non-violent and have no firearms in their home. Their two boys, as pre-schoolers, chewed their peanut butter sandwiches into the shape of pistols and began to shoot at one another. It's just built into us as males.

Jan told me recently that our boys decided to have a "tea party". I have no idea why. We've never had one here. But a tea party they had, on the back of a toy horse. It was very proper and polite. When it was over, they looked at one another and said, "OK, let's kill the horse!" Whereupon they pretended to dispatch said equine in a vicious manner. I don't know why, but little boys can tolerate only so much gentility.

Even our youngest, still 18 months, is known to me as "Elijah, agent of entropy", as he spends all of his waking hours attempting to undo every piece of the house that is put away, clean or organized. He is a tornado in a diaper; a classic boy.

So what can future parents do? Learn the special lexicon of boys. There are phrases and words that, if practiced repeatedly, might make raising boys more tolerable. Try these exercises. Stand in front of a mirror for 30 minutes repeatedly saying, "Quit it, quit it, quit it". Then shorten it to "Stop, Stop, Stop", then be real, and try, "Please, please, please". Move on to "Put down the knife" (substitute whatever you are concerned with, like cat, curling iron, household cleaner, brother, etc.). Do this over and over, increasing your time daily as you get into better parenting condition. And remember, there's a reason to use a mirror. Sometimes, when you are talking to boys, you might just as well be talking to yourself.

Make Way for the Girl

Many months ago, my wife Jan and I looked at each other in a small, dark room, by the light of an ultrasound machine. There was confusion and surprise on our faces. With Jan some 22 weeks pregnant we wanted to know the sex of the baby. Our friend Jim, a radiologist, looked at the screen and smiled, confirming what the technician had said. We looked more surprised. We looked at the screen again. It was true: a baby girl.

Let me set the stage. We have three boys. Sam, age 5; Seth, age 3; Elijah, age 13 months. We just assumed this one would also be of the XY variety. Never assume. Jan was speechless. I was out a filet-mignon and a two pound bag of M and M's that I had bet with some of my nurses, on my confident assertion that the next baby was also a boy. When I went to work and confessed they howled.

Jan and I spent the next several days trying to adjust. Now most people feel that family requires fairly even numbers of each sex. We weren't that family. We were comfortable with the testosterone-based home that we have enjoyed so far. My wife, the perfect mother for boys, is queen in her domain. She is adored by all of her men and rules with a benign hand. The idea of another female, a princess, a usurper, was a little disconcerting to her.

For me, somehow my identity had become bound up in being a father of sons. I know how to handle them. I know how to play knights and dragons; I know how to wrestle with toddlers and not incur permanent damage to my genitalia. I do not know how to play dolls, how to braid hair, or (God help the girl) how to match colors.

Our home is a place awash in boys. It is action figure central, with knights, cowboys, firemen, soldiers and super-heroes in

48

every room.   Plastic swords are prized possessions which accompany the children to bed.   At any moment, a ball or block may fly through the air to be hopefully intercepted before smashing a picture frame or a brother's forehead. It is a place of excitement.

It's also a place of the bizarre.   Like the day I found Batman tied to the banister as a prisoner of war with Robin and Flash standing guard.   Or the day a Cat-Woman figure was tied hand and foot to a small boat and left for dead.   One day my wife witnessed the boys playing drive-thru and ordering happy meals, chocolate milk with a side of bug-guts and monkey brains. Boys are wonderfully weird.

So it must be obvious that we were a little, well, uncertain about what to do with a girl.   But not just Jan and me; when we told Sam, he literally gasped and his jaw dropped. It was going to be an interesting time.

But then, time has a way of fixing everything.   And as the weeks passed we came initially to acceptance, then to excitement. My situation was helped by a little lavender outfit that said; "Daddy's little angel".   The boys have declared themselves to be the loyal knights to the new princess.   Jan's angst was, I believe, relieved by her resolve to raise a strong feminine woman leader, not a foofoo girl.   We will adapt and our world will now begin to glow with the pink decorations and toys we have needed for so long.

I am not an animal! I'm a parent...

Looking back on the week just past, I recall that I walked through the house early one morning and wondered how it was that I had failed to hear hand grenades exploding in every room. I realized, thanks to the toddler clutching my leg and screaming, that it probably wasn't explosives, but more likely my children who had wrought such havoc. I kicked a path clear, and stumbled to the kitchen, still encumbered by my 30-pound parasite.

It wasn't an especially difficult week. It was just another week in the world of parenting. A week in which the afore-mentioned toddler managed to spill an entire can of wood varnish on the living room rug, requiring hours of cleaning. It was a week in which my oldest ran a sewing needle entirely through his big toe and screamed for at least 20 minutes until I was able to remove it. A week in which even the animals conspired against us, by chewing up a new welcome mat and scattering its remains, along with a similarly mauled diaper, around the yard.

These days, parenting is no more or less difficult than it ever was. However, we have increased expectations, which make it seem harder. Every week yields a new study, or a new theory, on what we should be doing to, with or for our sons and daughters. Should we use day care or not? Should unhappy couples divorce, or stay together for the children? Do computers create little geniuses or little vegetables? We struggle to do our best, don't we? We struggle to make our children functional and happy. To keep them healthy, safe and well educated. To keep them from terminating themselves, as it appears all small children are programmed, lemming like, to do. We really try.

But it's just hard. It's hard to do the right thing all the time. It's hard not to yell. It's hard to be supportive and understanding when the two oldest are screaming at each other over who had the moldy, forgotten-until-this-moment bath toy first. I find it difficult to encourage independent thought and curiosity in my 18-month-old when he seems to be the source of all the entropy in the universe and systematically empties every drawer and container in the house so meticulously that I'm sure he has developed a schedule for it. But there's something harder.

The harder, perhaps the hardest part, is remembering who we are as individuals. In our fervor to be the best parents possible, we too often sacrifice ourselves. It's a noble martyrdom, the death of an individual person in exchange for the parent that rises from the ashes. And it somehow eases the strain of our daily failure in the entirely impossible task of perfect parenting. So we lie on the altar with a certain degree of satisfaction. But, important as selflessness is, it is equally important to remember who we were and who we are.

Sometimes Jan and I look back and reflect. We think of life before the children. We remember, vaguely, the flagrant luxury of sleeping late. We remember going to dinner without leaving piles of debris under the table, or searching for bottles under our chairs. We recall the pleasure of shopping without having to keep one another from picking up breakable items. We believe we led quiet lives of relative ease. Of course, back then we couldn't see it.

Things are different now. Our lives revolve around the three, soon four, other lives that are our charges. And we wouldn't change it for anything. That's not a cliché, but a fact. We love parenting. But we don't feel guilty that we are still individuals in need of lives. And we have come to the conclusion that the children need to see that truth. They need to know that their parents are more than maid and butler, more than cook and provider. That we have interests, that we have desires and talents: and that though our world may revolve around them, it is still our world.

Tonight Jan went to Greenville, SC, to see a production of Cyrano de Bergerac. I was making dinner for the monsters when she walked into the kitchen, wearing a black maternity dress and shawl that stopped me in my tracks. I looked at her in all her beauty and remembered that, though we may be parents, we remain a man and a woman, just doing our best to get it right.

Altar Call

An altar call is a fascinating thing. The congregation quietly sings the invitational from memory. The preacher softly compels saints and sinners alike to come to the altar for repentance or rededication. If he is like most pastors I have known, this is one of the high points of his week. It's a complex fusion of genuine love, advanced public speaking, high-pressure sales and a smidgen of drama class. As the minutes tick by, his plea transforms. Suddenly he becomes a rescuer in a life-boat. "Come on! Come and pray at this altar! This may be your last chance! You might wreck your car on the way home! Are you ready for eternity?"

The master of this complex choreography is a friend of mine. He is a scholar, educated at a premier university of the south. He is a preacher of rare depth, crystal clarity. But once the sermon is over, he moves stealthily into what must be one of his deepest passions. The music plays softly but when the final verse is almost complete he holds up one finger, arm stretched above his tall frame. It means "one more verse, just one more." And the congregation proceeds to sing one more verse or one more hymn, as many times as it takes for him to feel satisfied with the service. He is an artist and his medium is the human heart. I always feel a need to repent of something when he holds up that finger. But then, in the midst of my self-examination, my glancing up at the aisle to see how far it is to the altar, someone else steps out in front of me and I hear something like this: "Just as I am, without one plea, but that this pastor set us free…" Of course, that little blasphemy is probably one of the reasons I should respond to invitations from time to time.

My friend isn't the first pastor who has moved me to leave the pew and step to the front. Over the years I've seen plenty of soul shaking, heart squeezing altar calls. My father is an old school

United Methodist preacher in West Virginia. He learned his invitations during his upbringing and at Asbury Seminary in Wilmore, Kentucky, where political correctness runs into the hard wall of old-time religion. Even before he entered the ministry I was raised on sermons that made me feel like Jonathan Edwards' parishioners, that hell was heating up just below the pews. I've stood for altar calls that seemed they might last till evening worship. My grandmother was Free Methodist, later Nazarene. My bride and in-laws are from the Church of Christ. (Same invitation, no piano). I know whereof I speak.

I'm a South Carolina Southern Baptist now. I still experience the range of emotions that comes with the invitation. But over the years I have become just a bit impatient as I sing through multiple verses of "I surrender all". Worse, I sometimes fear that C. S. Lewis' demonic character, Screwtape, has made me cynical about the faithful few who consistently respond week after week. Fortunately I think I understand my emotions at last.

At this stage in my life my impatience is pragmatic. It stems from parenting. Many a Sunday my wife and I sit in the pew with our four darling offspring, age seven years down to 18 months, as they fidget, illustrate hymnals, beg for candy or rifle through our pockets and relieve us of our loose change. Other Sundays, we can be found riding herd on 10 to 15 others in nursery or children's service. When the second hand strikes 12, I'm ready to hand the little cherubs off to their biological guardians so that I can avoid having evil thoughts far worse than wanting the service to end.

Worse than impatience, however, has been my cynicism about the invitation; or perhaps more accurately, my cynicism about my fellow church members and their response to it. It took a long time for me to understand those parishioners who, for my entire life, have consistently gone to speak to the pastor, or kneel at the altar, at every service. As an impressionable youth I was certain that these folks were hands-down saints. Many were persons I had known for years, respectable and good. I felt less Godly when I sat in my pew while they courageously poured out their souls. I grew up and moved away but I have become aware that the same thing happens in every church that has an invitation. Methodist, Nazarene or Baptist, it's the same phenomenon. Sometimes they kneel, sometimes they don't. Sometimes they wipe away tears. Some cry every Sunday. I often thought that if I were a better Christian, I'd cry more too.

But then I figured it out and my cynicism was largely cured. Living as I do in South Carolina, in a small town, in the land of sumptuous Sunday spreads made by mothers, grandmothers and family owned restaurants, the answer came to me like an epiphany. (No blasphemy intended there). The same people who go to the altar Sunday after Sunday are doing it for the rest of us. They're leaning in and taking one for the team. They're jumping on the grenade. Like me, they know that "somethin' has got to be done", else the stove will catch fire or the lines at the cafeteria will be swollen with succinct Presbyterians and practical Lutherans.

Driven by a passionate love of fried chicken, macaroni and cheese, sweet potato casserole and sweet tea, these brave souls march down the aisle so that the pastor will have a tangible result on those Sundays when no one in the congregation has the desire or the willingness to be public about their soul's inadequacies.

On one level it's an act of respect toward a hard-working preacher, who might get discouraged if no one responded. Just as important, it's an act of true Christian charity toward the entire body of restless, hungry believers gathered under the roof of the church to worship the infinite Almighty for the Biblically prescribed 60 minutes.

I see them all differently now. The habitual confessors are an elite group, whose long practiced sincerity is an artistic match for the one finger held in the air for another verse. They are equally matched. Perhaps those good souls now believe in their hearts that they need that stroll, that shake, that embrace week after week. I'm sure that hundreds of preachers need them just as certainly.

Regardless of why or how they go about it, I'm grateful. Between wiggling toddlers, nursing babies and my own growling stomach, something has got to be done. I guess this week I'll have to go down myself. It's my turn. Maybe I can confess my impatience.

Last Call for Babies

Well, she's here. Our perfect princess was born; 8 pounds, 12.4 ounces, 20 inches long. She and her mother are doing great. We expect her to be our last child. Jan asked me not long ago; "Please, can I not be pregnant again?" She calculated that she has spent forty months pregnant since 1994. Considering it's 2001, that's a pretty titanic effort. I feel happy, because we have four wonderful children. I feel a bit sad, because I will not feel a child move within Jan's body again; nor will we will pick out names or newborn clothes. This may be the last time we go to a hospital for a purely joyous reason. But I also feel relief, a sense that the timing is right. As with all things, there is a season. And the season of having babies has passed.

Pregnancy is a thing that Jan and I have come to love. Easy for me to say since I haven't carried any children. But I have tried to be a part of it all, and we have shared much in the last seven years. We have shared hopes and dreams, changes in diet and appetite, fluctuations in schedule, alterations in physical appearance. We have rich memories. And we have artifacts, like some maternity clothes, that I will never be able to discard. I see my wife's face smiling, her hands resting on her full abdomen; the color and design of the outfits are fixed in my mind as surely as the color of her eyes and hair.

We have many memories of poignant times, like first finding out that we would have a child, and first hearing the heartbeat of each one. My favorite memories of being surprised by the sex of our first child; then seeing it displayed on the ultrasound screen with each of the others. And the incredible memories of the moments when, after pain and struggle, breathing and pushing, a child came forth into the world, a life in God's image, with both of our traits intermingled; a red-faced whimpering human, perfect in form, infinite in possibility, freshly emerged into the arms of parents whose love was as tangible as the child itself.

We tried to enjoy each pregnancy intensely; to catalogue the weeks and the changes. This time we explained to the children what was happening with their sister at each phase of development. We let them feel her move. We told them when she could hear them and learn her brother's voices even within the womb. We let them give their opinions about her name and smiled as they insisted on buying her presents. This pregnancy has been a family affair more than any other.

But the time has come to stop. Not because we haven't been in love with everything about having children. We have been and continue to be. It is simply time. Besides the battle is only just joined; we have decades of raising yet to do. We have all the joys and struggles of parenting still before us as we try to guide four young souls onto the paths of truth. But one part will pass behind us, just as other milestones have, like our first date these 17 years ago.

Looking back, I doubt we would have believed our eyes had we peeked through some portal to our future, from then to now. We might have laughed, or gasped, or shaken our heads. We are different people but the differences are not so profound. When we were younger, we had joys and trials, trips and dates, limited budgets, tests and job applications. Now our trials are things like sick children, tidal waves of laundry and sleeplessness. Our dates may be dinner and Wal-Mart, or bedtime stories and a movie rental set to the gentle background of softly breathing children. Parenting has only amplified the love that was already there.

By now, pregnancy and children are so much a part of who we are that they seem always to have been. They were and are the greatest adventures of our lives, the things that have shaped and defined us. They are the stuff of dreams and the content of the memories we will travel through for the rest of our days. God is good.

Parent Gift

It's funny how parenthood evolves. When our first child, Sam, was born seven years ago, we boiled nipples (the ones on the bottles, mind you), scrubbed bottles, uniformly warmed all of his food, tried to keep his hands clean at all times and so on. By number four, well let's just say that little Elysa has quite the immune system. As long as the things she puts in her mouth aren't decaying organic matter, we don't worry too much. She isn't alone. I just saw her two-year-old brother Elijah, lounging naked against a hound dog that smelled vaguely of week old skunk, while trying to force feed him dog chow. At least the child got a bath before bed.

But that evolution of parenting skills extends to consumer activity as well. Now that I have the perspective of my four children, I enjoy going to baby stores. I even get a kick out of those highly targeted specialty catalogs for "smart babies" or "overdressed babies" or any of dozens of other titles designed to pull in people susceptible enough to believe that their love for their children is predicated on nifty gadgets and high contrast, black and white infant mobiles.

When Jan and I were new parents with little Sam our own cuddly lab rat, we were occasionally duped. But not for long. Over the years that we have sailed the sea of parenthood we have thrown quite a lot overboard. We tossed cribs and bassinets, for example. Our babies climbed too early for bassinets and crib assembly is prone to induce profanity, as well as an unhealthy desire for liquor. And the list goes on. Catalogs and stores try and seduce parents with special bathtub seats, elaborate video monitoring systems, "must have" stuffed animals that sound like the placenta and tons of other things that may be good ideas but aren't essential to raising the little nippers.

Nevertheless I have a weakness. The thing that suckers me in is the toy department. I'm a child at heart and I love toys. I know they aren't absolutely necessary to parenting but I love to look at them, play with them and buy them for my children. Thank God my wife has good sense. I can't count the number of times I have come to her with a box in my hands at the store and explained how the enclosed item would delight our offspring, as well as making them stronger and smarter. She always calmly looked at it, looked at me, then shook her head. "What I see is a large box full of thousands of little pieces that will be all over my house when the children start to throw them at each other". "But…" "No!" she firmly says. And she's right. The catalogs are the same. I want to buy model rockets, trampoline like devices, grappling hooks, dartboards and everything I see because I imagine my kids enjoying them. Jan has good sense and vividly explains the sobering reality of my potential purchase.

But as I've played with the children lately I have realized a great truth about toys and it rings true at Christmas time also. We have a house full of toys but the one consistent fact is that the children want either Jan or I to play with them. And if we do the toys themselves seem suddenly irrelevant. They can be stick swords, matchbox cars or semi-deflated balls. The great truth is this: an interested parent is the greatest gift a child can have. A father or mother willing to play on the floor, uninterrupted by telephone calls, housework or any other distraction, is a toy of infinite price. That parent becomes magical and is instantly transformed into a wrestling partner, a monster, a wild animal, a jungle gym or any of thousands of other things created in the imagination of the child. My baby could care less about the bells, whistles, buzzes and flashing lights of the toys we so dutifully purchased for her. But when I enter the room, she wants to play.

And she will crawl up and down my body with peels of laughter until her little eyes glass over with fatigue.

As Christmas is nearly here too many parents will worry that they can't give their children enough. But they needn't fret. Because the greatest gift any parent can give their child is the most obvious. They can give themselves. Even Santa can't trump that.

Hope

I hate to be my children's physician. I do it with reservations. I'll treat the sore throat. I'll give breathing treatments for the wheezing. But sometimes I reach uncomfortable territory. On March 22, I entered just such a place when my 5-year-old, Seth, began drinking like he had just come in from the desert. He had Scarlet Fever. I assumed he was drinking because his throat was sore. But when he said it wasn't, and refilled his cup over and over, I knew it was time to look further. I was afraid of the obvious. So we went to the ED and checked his glucose. It was 608. A number I won't forget. He looked at me confused, uncertain why people he barely knew were sticking his fingers, drawing his blood. He was incredibly brave, but I imagine he believed it was temporary. That he would go home and life would be back to normal. That's what I kept hoping and praying. That's what I continue to hope and pray as we attempt to make his transition to diabetes as smooth as possible.

Diabetes sucks. There's no other way to put it. I hate everything about it, just as I'm sure Seth hates everything he so far understands about it. We have all cared for patients whose bodies have been decimated by this assault of glucose and retreat of pancreas. It's inane that a molecule so tiny can take a body and destroy it. But it's reality. And so I teeter back and forth, worried one day that he will have profoundly low blood sugars, or hypoglycemia, the next day that he will have terribly high sugars and develop blindness and renal failure. I need something like insulin to smooth my worry curve throughout the day. My wife Jan is keeping me calm. She handles stress with organization. My coping skills amount to enormous amounts of highly embellished anxiety. Seth, thanks to the prayers of many, has been heroic in his adjustment.

But trouble always has a lesson. In this case more than one. As a physician, I've learned a lot from this terrible time. And I think one of the most useful things I've learned is the importance of genuine compassion, having recently received so much of it. I thought I learned it from my kidney stone, or from the time Sam, then age2, was hospitalized with RSV and struggled to move air in and out of his little chest. I thought I learned it from all of the fevers and vomiting and other illnesses that Jan and I have faced over untold sleepless nights with four children. But apparently I didn't know much. For now, with a child facing a lifelong medical condition, I see more clearly the immense pain of parents whose children suffer. It is the worst pain a parent can experience short of the death of their child.

I remember meeting many parents of sick children down the years, with diseases both acute and chronic. I know there were times when I couldn't understand their hostility and frustration. I know that I tried to be the rational doctor and explain why they shouldn't worry. Many times, especially with the chronic illnesses, I explained that I was sorry, but that there really wasn't anything else we could do in the emergency department. I remember thinking that they were so difficult, and that I couldn't imagine being a pediatrician. There's a saying in medical school: "The kids are great, it's the parents that are tough!" I know why the parents are tough. The parents are tough, quite often, because the parents are scared to death.

What the parents see is their hope, their dream, their heart of hearts lying in a hospital bed suffering from a disease, or infection, that is often invisible. Their parents see their children being molested and abused by bacteria, viruses, glucose or the treasonous betrayal of their own DNA turned against them. What their parents cannot see is any way to stop it. If a person or animal were attacking their children, they would fight with their own lives. If it were a fire, they would cover their child with a blanket and run to the door. If their child were drowning they would swim to them and pull them to safety. But when their children are ill, parents are worse than powerless. They stand by the bed and stroke their children's hair; they fill hospital rooms with stuffed animals; and they wander the halls, wishing for normality and blaming themselves, either for being useless to take away the pain, or for the imagined belief that they caused their child's condition.

What they need, in super-therapeutic doses, is compassion. They need for someone to listen as they tell the story over and over. They need to sit with someone who understands their fear, and is willing to help them shoulder it for a while. In the book of Romans, St. Paul said we are to "mourn with those who mourn". Unfortunately, it's much easier once we have suffered a bit ourselves. It's easier to know the fear of a parent when one has become a parent. I didn't understand this until my children were born. And my grasp of compassion grew exponentially after March 22.

But compassion is only part of the equation. Because parents of sick and injured children need hope as well. It's so easy for us, with cool scientific clarity, to say that family members need to know the harsh reality, like the statistics on mortality and morbidity from the condition their little one is enduring. And even while this may be true, it isn't the whole truth. At least in the beginning, as parents are faced with the enormity of what life has dealt them, we need to offer some hope; even hope in the miraculous is better than no hope at all. And it isn't a lie. We have all seen things happen in medicine that defy science. It's OK to offer that hope, however fragile or fleeting.

One of the most wonderful things that happened to our family has been the outpouring of compassion and hope from friends, family and people involved with Seth's care. Two of the nurses in the emergency room where I work have children who were diagnosed this year with juvenile onset diabetes. They have been a wealth of information. In the beginning, when I was hardest hit, my partners offered me this treasure: "Maybe this is a temporary inflammation of his pancreas! I'm sure I've read about that!" And the endocrinologist we are seeing said to us: "Frankly, I expect a cure inside twenty years. The trick for now is to keep Seth from having too many lows or highs and keep his blood sugar on an even level. That way we protect him from complications and keep him healthy until the cure comes along!" The cure! Words I needed desperately to hear and believe.

Compassion and hope go hand in hand. I feel more of both these days. I have compassion for my own child; compassion for the parents of children who are ill. And I have special compassion for those children whose diseases have no cure, whose parents hope mainly in the mercy of Heaven.

I'm fortunate. My child has a disease for which a cure is almost tangible. He was born in a time when diabetes is not the worst disease imaginable. I have hope in the brilliance of scientists, hope in the fortitude of my child, hope that his mother and I can keep his world as normal as possible, and hope in the grace of his Creator.

And while we're on hope, I hope that those who read this will not face this trial. That everyone's insights can come from reflection rather than experience. As an old saying goes, experience is truly the bitterest way to learn wisdom.

Dog-shui

Last year was the Year of the Dragon, according to the Chinese Zodiac. But at our house the canine was and continues to be a dominant force. Our horoscope might well have read, "Your home will become a happy place; beware the destructive force of tooth, fur and fang". I suppose it all started in January 2000 when we acted in total disobedience to our better instincts and bought two puppies, litter-mates, from the animal shelter to give to the oldest boys as birthday gifts. We already had two large dogs. They were seven years old and well into the routine of things. They were past their destructive years and had settled down into comfortable worthlessness, barking occasionally when blowing leaves disturbed their sleep.

The new puppies, Max and Wendy, were a delight. Part hound, part who knows what, they were soft and sweet; everyone was in love with them. Although I have become less of an animal lover over the years, I felt heartfelt affection for the little fur-balls. That is until they went outside and discovered the meaning of destruction. Inside, behind their gate, they weren't so bad. There wasn't much to dismantle. Outside a whole new world appeared ripe for cataclysm.

All puppies are demolition experts. But Max and Wendy raised it to a fine art, going so far as to climb serious obstacles, at significant heights, to tear open garbage bags and eat diapers, so that the exposed absorbent material looked like piles of sleet on the driveway. They chewed on the wood siding of the house. They dug up plants. They rolled logs around the front porch at midnight. They were bulldozers with fur. But then the havoc spread from inanimate objects to animate. My two other dogs had been known to run down a possum or squirrel now and then. But with the help of their two youthful accomplices, the list grew longer and began to look like a zoology exercise. We had the normal ex-rats and squirrels. But now we had former groundhogs, prior-birds and several other bits of fauna, all from the eight acres surrounding the house.

Sadly, Wendy was killed by a car. We all mourned; even Max. But in tribute to his sister, he raised his level of devastation to new heights. That's really when I began to believe in Dog-Shui.

Feng Shui, of course, is all the rage these days. It is a Chinese system of establishing harmony and function in one's dwelling. It takes into account such factors as balance, color and geometry to make a place more spiritually and intellectually pleasing. Fair enough for people. Who would have suspected the same thing in dogs?

As I picked up thousands of bits of shredded paper and plastic for the fiftieth time, I began to see inside Max's mind. I imagined him looking at the house, pacing about and saying to himself, "what this yard needs today is paper. Where did I see some? Oh yeah, the dog food bag in the garage! I'll just shred it, put a few large pieces on the primroses, and everything will be fine!" On other days, he seems to feel that unraveled bits of welcome mat really represent the tone necessary for dog happiness. Wood, fabric, metal or plastic, Max is an abstract artist who works easily in any medium.

I'm sure people just think we're trash. Whenever the UPS truck comes down the drive, I'm afraid of what the driver might find; clean up as I may, the next day is a new adventure in Dog-Shui. But the December/January raccoon was the clincher. Max felt that we needed taxidermy. Or maybe he was creating some dog diorama. At any rate, poor Rocky met his maker at the hands/paws of the dogs and Max felt he belonged in the yard well after his untimely death. He would appear in various positions in the yard, sometimes prone, sometimes supine, sometimes in a peaceful fetal position that looked almost natural, except for the notable absence of movement and breath. He was sort of a furry Stalin. Fortunately, it was very cold, so we didn't have a 'scratch-and-sniff' raccoon carcass.

When friends brought us food after the baby was born, I asked if they had to step over the raccoon. They politely pretended they hadn't seen it. I hope they just thought our yard was an idyllic, Disney-like place where animals scamper (and repose) harmoniously. I didn't try to explain the Dog-Shui. Max just smiled.

Father Duty

The plain, pretty young woman I was treating had bronchitis. Beside her lay a baby a few months old. I turned to the man with her, the child's father, and made some reference to her as his wife. His response was prompt: "No, we ain't married." "Why haven't you married this girl?" I asked, ever the busy-body. He squirmed and said, "Well, marriage ain't something you just jump into!" "You mean, like having a baby?" I asked.

The mother smiled between coughs and left the ER. What I wanted to ask was, "Look at this fine young woman who was willing to have your child! Are you waiting for something better? Do you think, my scrawny little friend, that a bikini clad model is going to suddenly appear and sweep you away? Is this good girl not good enough for you?"

Maybe it wasn't any of my business. But now that I'm raising three sons who may be fathers, and one daughter who may be a mother, I feel that this issue is my business. When I see un-married women with children, I don't feel any puritanical condemnation for them. What I feel is worry for their loneliness and struggles. What I feel is disappointment that men can be so uninvolved in the lives of their women and children. What I feel is shame for those men who have extricated themselves from responsibility; exiled themselves from love, family and the future that child represents.

I'm sure that some of the women I see in the hospital are single mothers by tragedy or choice. Some may be widows. Some wanted a child and couldn't find the right relationship. For others, the father of their child was cruel, violent or addicted, and they felt it safer to be away from him. But I'm equally sure that most women who have given a man their bodies and hearts, and in the process a child, are women who want a commitment.

The excuses men make have the sound of sincerity. "I want to be able to give you a nice ring. I want to be able to take care of you. I want to be sure." Those are all proper answers. Before the baby. Afterward, they are stalls and hedges. Women want to know that their child's father will be there. They want a promise not so easily broken, a presence not so readily abandoned. Something like "till death do we part".

They don't need a $10,000 dress and a $20,000 diamond. All they want is the promise that comes with the dress and ring. They want their man to say "I love you, I do, I will", to them and to their baby. Who, even if poor, will do his best for them both. They want someone to trust and lean on in troubles.

Men often want only the moment and then the escape route. Men want the 'option' for a different woman when the burdens of the first become too great. When the cute dresses and tight jeans are replaced by maternity-wear and evenings involve less dancing and fun, more rocking and feeding.

But men themselves have been deceived and under-educated. Movies, television and popular men's magazines have taught them to fear the woman who wants a child. They have been indoctrinated to believe that their happiness and greatness cannot involve children or the 'dull' women who want them. Just as devastating, many of the men who abandon their children were themselves abandoned or ignored by their own fathers.

What they are missing is their highest calling and the reason for many of their own drives and abilities. The desire for romance and sex is connected to the care of a woman and the creation of children to carry one's genes and dreams down the ages. The strength to stand and fight exists for men to defend their women and children. The need for work and skills gives men the drive to provide for their families. Men are programmed for fatherhood. But they have exchanged their destiny for simple biology.

As we struggle with an epidemic of young, un-wed mothers, we have to address birth control and abstinence. But in order to change it, we have to teach young men accountability, duty, honor and most of all, love. So that when they lie down with a woman, they are ready (and willing) to be responsible for a child. So that they see the child they created not as her child, but as theirs.

Christmas Photos

Jan, her sister Julie and I spent yesterday evening putting up Christmas decorations with the children. It's Sam's seventh Christmas, though just barely. He was two days old on his first. A squeaking, wriggling elf sent to his mother and me from God. If Santa had brought him it would have taken two days more and that would have been unacceptable (according to his mother).

His siblings are experiencing their fourth, third and first Christmases and we are all excited. I can see them beginning to develop traditions, things stored in their memories that mean Christmas to them and that they expect to do each year. For one, they have a tree in their room for the season. A small tree that they decorate themselves. It's artificial and last night we left the lights on so it could be their own multi-colored night light. I still remember lying under my tree as a child, looking up at a tiny universe of decorations and a varied spectrum of glowing bulbs.

As we decorated, I dutifully pulled out the video-camera. I filmed everyone until they began to look at me with slight annoyance, except for my 11-month-old daughter, who should be a model. But as I filmed I was aware of the reality of filming and pictures. Who will view these tapes? Will the children sit around with their own children and look at decades old video-tapes, then reminisce about these magical times? And who will keep the photo-albums we so meticulously store and update? Will the four children divide them among one another? And what after them? Can I hope that my grandchildren, or great grandchildren will care for them like the treasures they are to Jan and me? One of my friends once said of video-cameras, "Why should I film my children all the time? So I can watch them in my old age and cry because they are not children anymore?" A good question.

I am always disturbed by this idea especially at Christmas. I am always obsessed with little memorabilia. With locks of hair from first haircuts, with clothing I loved to see the children wear. I am totally sentimental about those precious toys with which we played for hours in the warm corners of the house, as winter blew outside. But not long ago Jan gave me a hard realization about all of this, as I lamented not taking enough photos of the children on an outing. She said, "You know, the pictures are only for us after all. Enjoy the time you have, don't worry about photos."

As always, she was right on track. Memories are the greatest videos, the most wondrous photos. I won't stop taking the ones on film because I will look at them one day and I'll keep them like diamonds so that down the years, our descendants will know a little about us. But if they don't and if all the images are lost, along with everything I ever wrote about them, it won't be so horrible. I know, because good memories are translated into loving actions, into happy, healthy children, into marriages that become legends of devotion and joy in family histories.

What do I know of my ancestors? I know little beyond the 19th and 20th centuries. But my family was filled with love and devotion, with strength and purpose, and at each increment these fires were stoked by individual persons' memories of goodness, passion, laughter and play. I have no pictures of my family at Christmas in 1600 or 1800, but I know it was good and that there was laughter and decorations, good food and happiness. I know this because I experienced these things and traditions are the tangible remnants of lost memories.

So this year I'll try to worry a little less about pictures and video. I'll keep the cameras nearby but I'll try to store up in my mind the delights of the season, from the simple taste of good chocolate to the bright blue eyes of baby's first morning opening packages. Because there, dear ones, are where the most enduring images can be found.

Bathroom Break

I wish that I knew how many times my family has repeated this scene. We enter a restaurant with our four children. We sit down, order food, and upon arrival of the food, someone needs to go potty. This is a behavior exhibited by all of my offspring, but Seth, age four, is the master. Something about restaurants, as simple as entering one, affects his body in such a manner that a trip to the rest-room is critical to further enjoyment of the meal. It doesn't matter if he relieved himself at home twenty minutes prior. The facilities at the restaurant beckon him, like a little lemming to the sea.

Consequently, I've been on a tour of public rest-rooms across the country. Seth has been my tour guide since he was potty trained. He is an aficionado. His love of rest-rooms has led us to a number of conclusions. One, a nice facility is a blessing that can be found in most department stores, some restaurants, the occasional fast-food establishment and virtually no gas station anywhere. We have considered writing a book: "Pottys of America", 1997 to 2001, by Seth and Edwin Leap.

Furthermore we have discovered that our fellow men are generally pigs, they cannot maintain anything approaching sanitary behavior in public. As a father, I've considered carrying a gallon of bleach wherever I go. We have also noted that most toilets are uncomfortably high for a toddler. The average stall is also uncomfortably tiny, as we have noted when going to the bathroom with all three brothers. At those times, the handicapped stall is essential. But there are unfortunate down sides. Wrestling matches have erupted without warning. Worse, Elijah, age two, is enthralled by floor drains and lies down on the tile to peer into them. This is disgusting. I think I'll start soaking him in bleach too.

But more than the technicalities of bathrooms, more than the enlightening insights into modern architecture, plumbing and toilet paper quality, we have discovered something far-more grand. That our time together, whether seated at a dinner table or simply chatting in the rest-room stall, is precious. It's easy to get annoyed when we get up and go. As an adult, I sometimes just want a relaxing dinner with family and friends. Occasionally, I grump at him or roll my eyes at his mother (who rolls hers back at me as only a wife can). However every time I go, I am rewarded.

What typically happens on our little toilet adventures is that Seth sits down, holds my hands as I crouch on the floor and we talk. Sometimes our talks turn to theology, like our recurrent discussion of his dog Wendy, killed by a car. "Papa, someday we'll see Wendy in Heaven!" Other times it's deeper still. "Papa, did you know that God and Jesus are the same person?" Occasionally we talk about dreams for the future. "Papa, will you go into space with me someday? I want to be an astronaut and a doctor!" And best of all, it can simply be a moment of effusive love. "I love you, you're the best Papa in the world!" I love you too, Seth.

I have learned that my life is full of moments of such potential delight. But they require that I think more as a child, less as an adult. To my children every moment is a time of wonder, every place conceals an adventure waiting to be discovered. My day, with time set aside for writing or other grown up pursuits, will often be better spent wrestling with Seth, assembling Legos with Sam, racing toy cars with Elijah or playing peakaboo with pink clad baby Elysa. These things remind me how I meandered through childhood and how good it felt. A trip to the bathroom, an hour or two of unscheduled play, may seem inconvenient disruptions of my schedule. But if I let my children be my guides, they always show me the path to unexpected pleasure. And I am always better for the trip.

Halloween

We received our first Halloween catalogs some time around July or August. Since that time, my boys have been frantically going through them to decide on this year's costumes. It's only one night, but in the world of small children it has much the same weight as picking a prom dress does to a teenage woman. It has to be just right. It has to say something about the wearer.

My boys gravitate consistently to ninja and knight costumes. In the past, super heroes have been the theme. We even had cute costumes occasionally, like lions with huge manes, which we forced on them as toddlers. But now, even three-year old Elijah is past that, and feels that his personality requires a costume that is a little bit dangerous. He wants to carry plastic daggers and swords like his big brothers. I guess it doesn't make sense to go out into a dark night, filled with pretend monsters, without being adequately armed.

But to my children, Halloween is more than a costume. It's a mood. That's why they were so excited to decorate our home with light up haunted houses, ghosts, vampires, mummies and spiders. Halloween is a time when little ones love well-confined fear, and when terror is indistinguishable from delight.

I'm fascinated by this, but not surprised. When I was a child, Halloween was one of the grandest nights of my kid year. I lived on a rural road where we could trick or treat for hours, much longer than the tame, post-modern, subdivision-safe 60 minutes allotted by law. We roamed long into the night. As long as a porch light remained on, we knocked on the door. We set off fireworks. We ambushed one another by flashlight. It was grand. The little valley where we lived captured the cool, moonlit night in magical ways. By the time we came home, we were cold, thrilled, and stuffed with candy. We had bravely ventured into the night, successfully avoided being nabbed by evil creatures or clubbed by enthusiastic but frightened friends, and returned victorious. On Halloween, we wallowed in the delicious pleasure of one special, scary night.

I'm convinced that this desire for fear and for mystery is the secret of the season. Sure, dressing up is fun. But the little ones, and we big ones, love Halloween because it reminds us that the world is still a place in which some things are unknown. It takes us back in time, before science had ready explanations for so many things, and when our ancestors concocted their own answers to the unexplained noises, the seldom seen creatures, and the beautiful, untouchable lights in the evening sky. It reminds us that we are both vulnerable to the unknown and capable of facing it. It lets us slip briefly into another world for just a little while.

Of course, the origins of Halloween aren't exactly pleasant. I know some who refuse to participate, because it harkens back to the horrible ages when our ancestors were guilty of human sacrifice and other terrible acts, all to appease merciless gods and spirits. I respect this devotion to consistent spiritual truth. Besides, terrible things happen in the name of fun and real beasts (mostly of the human variety) still roam the starlit streets at the end of October.

But most of us aren't drawn to Halloween because we are evil or misled. I believe that our spirits are simply starving for wonder. We need the numinous, the inexplicable. We need more in our spiritual lives than moral platitudes. We need to remember that even God seems to delight in both tenderness and power, sunlight and storm. And that our love of dark nights as well as clear days is only a reflection of our maker whose acts include creating everything in the exploding darkness of nothing, warring with renegade angels, flooding the world in anger, raising the dead, sacrificing himself under dark skies to protect us from the fires of Hell, and rising from a cold tomb to new life.

We humans need more than goodness to keep our souls alive. We need wonder, healthy fear, mystery and the delight of the battle of good versus evil. And in some ways, though I'll be pilloried for this, I think that Halloween gives us just a taste of these things for one knight, ninja and monster-filled evening a year.

The Screaming Hornets

A hike in the woods is great therapy for rambunctious children. So, a few weeks ago I put baby Elysa in her backpack, lined her three brothers up and off we went into the woods around our house. About one fourth of a mile from our home, through dense pines, is a logging yard. Usually abandoned, it is an area of open dirt with ample rocks and dirt clods, small piles of timber cuttings and various logging roads that take off into the woods in various directions. It's a magical place for children, so off we went.

Our hike out was uneventful except for a few scrapes from briars. Autumn was settling upon us and the evening was cool in the shade. We played, caught a lizard, watched the dogs romp around and then decided it was time to return for dinner.

On the way back, however, the excitement began. Taking a short cut in front of our house we marched through tall grass and brush, over-grown since the trees were timbered away a few years ago. Half-way down the path I began to hear an insect buzz around me. Not your average horsefly, this was something annoyed and determined. Unable to spin and face it due to the infant on my back, I twisted and turned until it landed on my neck and stung me with the calculated precision of a cruise missile. Forgetting the little ears around me, I uttered some profanity and realized we all needed to begin a hasty hustle to home.

For better or worse the boys didn't hear me. They were too busy screaming, lying on the ground and trying to swat away the white-faced hornets that had begun to swarm around all of us. I began to scream too. "Run! Get up and run!" I felt like the veteran sergeant in a WWII movie, pulling his soldiers to cover while carrying a wounded pal on his back, bullets zipping all around.

I picked up two-year-old Elijah and knocked a hornet from his lower lip. Trying to get to his older brothers, all of us still howling in pain and terror, I clothes-lined the baby no less than three times, resulting in bruises on her nose and neck, made worse by the hornet sting next to her ear. In what seemed like forever but was probably less than one minute, we were out of the woods and running to the safety of our house like Satan himself were behind us.

Some hugs from Mama and Aunt Julie eased the screaming. Popsicles and ice eased the pain. And with a Batman video in the VCR all was quiet at last. What a day. Later, laughing and licking our wounds (everyone had been stung), we decided to call our merry band "The Screaming Hornets". I told the boys they were brave and that after some good autumn freezes we would collect the hornets' nest and sell it to someone for decoration. They get the money. Everyone has recovered nicely except for Elijah, who still sees "bugs" where there aren't any.

We learned some lessons. Most notably, I explained that when Papa says run they should drop everything and run. Also, we learned which trail is temporarily off-limits, since I went back to look and the nest is some two feet tall and right by the path. The boys won't be going back in the woods any time soon.

But the event reinforced a truth that I always knew. That is my children respond best to the crises in their lives when I tell them that they are heroic. The hornets were scary and painful but now they're just part of the family legend. We learned that we could handle the fear even the discomfort and laugh about it. I remember the time that Seth, then age 3, pushed Sam, then age 5, into the deep end of a pool. I was in the water nearby and watched it happen. Sam, having had swimming lessons kicked to the surface, spit the water from his mouth and screamed. But all the family praised him for his skill in swimming and his courage in coping. By that night he might as well have been a Navy Seal. He looked back on the event with a sense of pride at his survival.

I want childhood to be a time of wonder and innocence for my little ones. But it must also be a time of preparation in which Jan and I teach them the fortitude that they will need in life. I don't know when they will have to apply that strength. I only know that eventually, they will.

Nature Love

All relationships are tumultuous at times. Whether it's the interaction between parent and child or husband and wife, relationships cycle like ocean waves and we are alternately crazed with frustration or mad with joy. One such relationship of mine has recently cycled back into delight. It is my complicated, frustrating relationship with nature.

I have remarked before that I love South Carolina. I love the people, the culture, the landscape and a thousand other things that define my home here. What I do not love is summer. In spite of the fact that many from my home state of West Virginia would give up important body parts to live here under eternally sunny skies, I find myself anxious as summer rolls around.

I rub my nose and eyes and speak unkindly of nature when my yard blooms in February. I mourn a little when it becomes clear that taking a jacket in the car is wishful thinking. I look up into the sky and roll my eyes the first mornings in late spring when I can feel the heat building and the insects are already agitated by 9 am. I cover my ears when the weather announcer says of mid summer: "Looks like another beautiful day out there! Not a cloud in the sky for the next week at least! High 90's and clear. Get out there and enjoy it!" It may be a character flaw. It may be some deep-seated problem in my psyche that makes me prefer rain and cool to clear and hot. It's like an inverse seasonal affective disorder. Whatever the reason, I feel that nature turns on me in the summer.

The heat of summer here feels like nature is yelling at me. It seems she is dissatisfied with my activity level and is insisting that I go outside and be broiled to prove myself worthy of the gift of her intensity. She's nagging. "Get up and do something! The yard needs to be cut! Pull ticks off of the dog! And put on some shorts! You look like a flounder!" I used to bow my head and obey: "Yes dear." Now, as I've grown older, I have begun to be passive aggressive. What else is there? Yell at the sun and people call a mental health professional to evaluate you. So, I turn my back. I stay inside during the peak of her wrath, going out only in the evening when she isn't as loud. I think unfaithful thoughts, fantasizing about cooler places, scanning the paper for highs and lows in places like Saskatchewan. High 60, low 45. I close my eyes and dream as the children play with the water hose, their only solace in the South Carolina blast furnace.

She's made me less fun for them, you know. I don't run and play very well when I feel heat stroke creeping up on me. I sit on the porch. I may chase fireflies at night but my daylight playfulness really sinks when it's hazy, hot and humid. Fortunately for me, even my children are afflicted. Their Northern European lineage betrays them. "Can we come inside?" they plead, their faces flushed, their hair matted. By end of summer, they don't want to go out at all. I suppose it's like living in Alaska. There, you stay inside for the winter. Here, it's the opposite.

In short, I've been angry at nature since she summer arrived. She could have cooled things off if she wanted. She could have rained but until recently, she refused. She's been in quite a mood. Fortunately as in every relationship, it's time for the upswing. It's time for us to speak again. I know because she's finally listening, acknowledging my complaints. I guess she can't sustain her summer energy forever. I can tell because the nights are nicer. Not much, but just enough. Her mood is changing. We're speaking again as we pass one another. She touches my face in the evening. Her fingers and her breath are just the slightest bit cool on my face. She's flirting.

Consequently, I'm spending more time with her. I'll run in the yard with the children. I'll walk in the evening with my wife. I'm willing to hear nature's side of the story. She's demure again, whispering in my ear, telling me to be patient. The end of summer is foreplay. Before long we'll actually make up. And nature and I will be in love all over again in the cool, clear autumn.

Pulling The Wagon

I remember when my firstborn son Sam, now age seven, was only one or two years old. I could pull him all day long in the blue, plastic wagon that we bought. As soon as he was old enough I would load him into it and run as hard as I could up the steep drive that led to our home. Summer or fall, winter or spring, we would race up that hill and around our circular, shaded drive, past pine and holly, past honey-suckle and mountain laurel, dogs running alongside. Sam would laugh until he couldn't breathe and I would run until I couldn't either. It was break-neck, reckless and grand. Occasionally on fast turns at the bottom of the circle, gravity would rule and he would sprawl out. He'd cry a minute, then get up and clamber back into his little chariot. We could spend an afternoon that way. Just as we could spend long stretches of time running in circles with him held in my arms as he pretended to be Batman, a dragon, or some other flying creature other than a flying little boy. I remember because he was light and I felt strong. I was king of the universe because I had my son (my son!) in my arms and we had nothing but time before us.

And then came Seth, two years younger. I was king of the universe because I could put two little boys in that wagon and run up and down hills while they laughed just as they still do when they play together. I could pick them up simultaneously and run through the yard, hoist them into trees, or up onto slides at the same time. I measured my age with my perceived strength. Father of two sons, I was the strongest man alive.

And then there were three. When Elijah came along I was still Hercules. The wagon was getting crowded. But I could still pull it while doing wind-sprints along the flat part of our drive at the top of the circle. I always thought of it as a kind of stress test. If I could do that and have no chest pain, no gasping for air, then my heart was just fine. Of course my heart was really in the wagon behind me. The laughter of three boys was all the fuel I needed to sail across the concrete. Occasionally they would spill out into the yard or pavement together, arms and legs flying. A few scratches, maybe, but still more joy for all of us. Picking up and comforting three wounded boys was a trick made easier with the help of a good backpack. With one behind and one on each hip, I was invincible.

Until there were four. Of course Miss Elysa, the baby of the family, has never put up with any competition or neglect. When the wagon rolled out, its wheels sagging, she would climb in with the certainty that she was entitled to the first and last ride and every one in between. Four presented a slightly different problem. I thought we needed another wagon. But it wasn't just numbers. The problem was that in addition to adding more bodies, those bodies grew. Suddenly the little babies I could pull and carry all day added height and weight. We left that magical house with the hidden drive when they children were seven, five, three and one. It was time. They were approaching critical mass and the wagon was ready to retire. But subtly the message to me was that I was a little weaker; a little older.

It's a cruel thing that happens to parents. Time, which seems so unreal, so contrived, catches up with us. Wagons wear down. The t-shirts the children wore look smaller and the stains on them are from long forgotten ice-cream cones. It seems unfair that at every step of the way our children move forward at a pace that we can scarcely match. I can't pull them all in the blue wagon forever. Besides, our new house has gravel, not pavement, on the drive. The tired blue wagon sits in the back yard, sometimes used by the children to haul rocks or brush. A thoroughbred too old to race, hitched to the plow in its twilight. I can't imagine throwing it out. I think it will just stay here as a beloved artifact.

But I am resolved to keep up the spirit of the wagon as long as I can. We have a newer, smaller wagon and we have a wheelbarrow. If I can't pull or push all of them, I can do it one at a time. And when that becomes too difficult, they'll be too big for wagons anyway. I can run with them though. And when they run too well and their hearts and lungs are too powerful for mine, I can walk with them. And that should last a very, very long time. But when it doesn't, I can sit and talk to them. I hope that I can keep pace with their minds for as long as I live. And if I can't at least they'll talk to me. We have an intimacy- that need for one another's company- that was forged in the delirious wonder of wagon rides and wrestling matches in leaves, of hikes and bedtime stories. So if I'm old and if I'm confused and demented, I know that their voices will be a comfort to an old man and will take me back to days of blue wagons and green hillsides, fig trees in the yard and scraped knees on the pavement. I suspect they'll be pushing, pulling and carrying me by then.

In the end of it all, I'll simply go on and wait for them in the place where summers are endless and I have a strength that never fades away. And when they meet me there, I'll be waiting in the cool autumn air, wagon at the ready, and off we'll go forever.

Cloning Cats

I recently read about a woman who had paid $50,000 to have her dead cat cloned. Her cat cloned! I appreciate love for a pet. I really do. But just as they used to say, "cocaine is God's way of saying you have too much money", so are cloned cats. Besides, for $500 a starving college student could be shown a picture of the beloved deceased cat and would find a near carbon copy inside 24 hours (though not necessarily by legal means).

Of course cats are special. I've had some great cats in my day. My children asked me how many cats I had owned (or that had owned me as some might say). The tally ran to around ten or twelve. Each of them was unique. I remember that some were black and some tabby and some calico. One was mute (unless you stepped on his tail in the night when he inexplicably screamed like a banshee). Several have had chronic cough and one was perpetually covered in green nasal drainage because of his apparent allergy to humans.

I had a Siamese that was very protective of me when I was ill as a child. One was a college campus orphan that moved from apartment to apartment until I lost track of him. A few had catnip addictions that left them furry, stoned little 'nip-heads', rolling about the floor completely out of their brains. At least two met unfortunate and violent ends. Once I saw three of our cats chasing a very embarrassed dog out of the yard.

One of these delightful felines fell down an abandoned well under my father's church and was heard faintly meowing beneath the floorboards. He was rescued (by the fire department) in a vertical reversal of the cliché 'cat in the tree'. My med-school cat showered with me; but then realized that my wife (then girlfriend) was nicer and more indulgent than I and moved in with her. My wife's cat, rescued from cruel rock-throwing children on a road trip, did not shower with her but leered at her while she showered, so that she wondered if he were a re-incarnated voyeur. In the end, all of them were a pleasure. But none of them, I mean none of them, would merit $50,000 to bring back to the planet.

The thing is, we just obtained two new kittens for our youngest children. And for a total bill of around $100 we have two fully functional, standard issue male cats. Claws, teeth, fur and superior attitudes included. The only parts they lack are the ones left behind at the vet's office when they were neutered. None the worse for the wear, they do all the things that cats have always done. They run madly across the floor on their velvety soft feet and smack into the wall trying to stop.

They swat Legos and Barbie paraphernalia all over the living room. They eat string. They climb onto the table in search of food. They use the litter box dutifully. They sleep on the children's heads at night. They wrestle and fight. They purr and collapse in exhaustion alongside one another. All for a C-note. And despite the availability of cloning technology, the regular feline factory is still churning out cats at a remarkable rate. I have no doubt that one million cats will be born on judgment day.

Of course technology is a great thing. But if I were going to monkey around with cat genes I'd do something beside make another one that looked exactly like the first. For example I'd give them opposable thumbs. "Open your own cat food you arrogant fur-bag!" I'd make permanent, non-shedding fur. How about a sleep switch? Maybe I'd try to engineer a cat that loved nothing better than staying on the floor; a kind of 'afraid of heights scaredy-cat'.

One of our new cats has a better idea. He belongs to our daughter Elysa. His name is (appropriately) Barbie. He wears a flowered collar. There weren't any girl cats available so he became one by default, because the princess wanted a girl cat. Barbie suggests to cat cloning scientists that he would like a new pair of gonads. Maybe then the feminine name and foo-foo collar might be more bearable.

And as for cloning new cats, Barbie says that if someone gives him new parts and an open door he'll make you some new cats; no problem at all.

Rescue Heroes

I love to watch my four children play as much as I love to play with them. We have a wonderful time, outside or in, as we play with knights, super-heroes, cars and blocks. We have intense sword-fights with sticks followed by my aerobics exercise session as I pull them in their wagon. Play is the work of children and it is important that they be content in it. I am told by my wife, a counselor, that play therapists use this most natural act of the young to help discover what issues trouble their growing minds and help them navigate the fears and sorrows that sometimes entangle them.

Recently, I've noticed some interesting choices in the things they play with most. Interesting, that is, in light of the events of 11 September, 2001. They have been playing a great deal with toys called "Rescue Heroes". Made by Fisher-Price (God love 'em), these virtually indestructible toys are firefighters, paramedics, rangers, police officers, construction workers, divers and others. The legend that the company has built around them is that they use their courage, skills and specific tools to rescue persons in danger. They have heavy construction equipment, grappling hooks, litters, police motorcycles, helicopters, boats and tons of other accessories with which to affect their adventures. And they have a tower, which is their base of operations. How about that?

My wife and I have observed the children, especially my six and four year old sons, creating disasters and rescue operations around the base of this tower. Sadly, they've seen just enough of the news coverage of the World Trade Center to have a vague idea of the tragedy. And we've tried to be forthright but reassuring when we speak to them. I think that they're acting out their concerns, then imposing control on them, with the actions of their toys. In a sense, I'm pleased.

The thing is, the world is full of anti-heroes. Outstanding imitators, children have learned in recent decades to emulate persons, or groups, of questionable character and dubious contribution to society. Whether professional athletes, actors, politicians, popular musicians, fictional villains or any of dozens of others, many of the people whose lives seem to draw the attention of our most precious resource are persons we would rather not have over for dinner. But now, with events being what they are, we can do a little re-direction.

Now we can point to persons who, despite their lack of fame or fortune, did great things in life and in death. We can lift up the police officers, firefighters, paramedics, doctors and nurses, construction workers and others who worked selflessly and sometimes to their own demise in order to help their fellow men and women in New York and Washington, DC. We can point to the soldiers, sailors and airmen who aided in rescue, who guarded the population with weapons ready and who now stand bravely on the brink of war. When my children hear an F-16 scream overhead and express concern, I can tell them "Don't worry honey, that's just someone who is protecting us!"

Ever since my father went to Vietnam when I was four years old I have held him up as heroic. And I have continued to feel that way about anyone who serves my country in time of crisis. Like my boys, when I was a child I loved toy soldiers and GI Joe action figures. To this day I stop in the aisles of toy stores and admire them. Not because I adore destruction or death. But because I learned to hold in high esteem those who served others in dire times with courage and self-abnegation.

When I see my children play "Rescue Heroes" and watch their characters save one another from danger, I see hope for a generation. Maybe one of the crops harvested from the disaster can be a renewed respect for those who risk and serve. If we desire greatness and valor in our young people, if we see duty and patriotism as virtues worth teaching, now is the time. The stories are ripe for telling as the real life rescue heroes continue their acts of bravery and will no doubt be called upon to perform even more.

The Museum of Memory

My wife Jan sat across the table from me at a little restaurant called Café Rendezvous. Although we have been married for 11 years, that's only part of our history. We dated for six years before our marriage. Three states, four children, five cars and one mortgage later and there we were. Intent on dinner and a play at the local community theater, we were late by the time we showered, dressed, kissed each child, and left them with the sitter. We decided to enjoy a long dinner. Every parent knows what a joy it is to eat while someone brings you food and drink, without having to hold a child in a chair, fill cups or clean spills. It was great.

Our conversation was light. Then Jan turned her head and asked me pointedly, "Do you remember what we did on our second date?" The "husband in danger" alarm sounded. My blood pressure rose to supply oxygen to my frantically searching brain. Cerebral files were accessed, key-words searched, cardboard boxes of neurons dusted off and examined in nanoseconds. Honesty prevailed. "No, I don't", I said, fearing that our second date had been some critical moment in the development of our relationship. "Me neither," she said and smiled. Whew.

But as my heart rate slowed, we began to reminisce. We decided that we were probably on our 1200th date, give or take 50. This was based on calculations and estimates involving average numbers of dates per week before and after children, as well as money and time available to date during school and residency, etc. 1200 sounded just about right. Looking around us we realized that some of the couples in the restaurant probably were on date 4000 or more.

Despite the years, I looked in my wife's face and saw the same woman I had fallen in love with in college. Time changes us but not so much. Love makes us like those persons who reclaim art. We can look at the picture, the image of the person we love and see behind gray hair, lines in skin, changes in body shape, hair style, clothing and thousands of little determinants of externals. When we do we see clearly the one we love best; the masterpiece is clear to our trained eye.

It's as if time is a thing that exists only marginally. It is a force to be sure. It wears upon us with every passing year. It degrades us inside and out until it finally causes our bodies to visit us with the ultimate betrayal of death.

But despite the effects of time, despite its constant erosion of our temporal existence, we are beyond it and in some ways impervious to it. Time cannot, of its' own accord, destroy our memories. Memory is a museum, an art gallery of the intellect and heart, the halls of which we may walk at any time. Unless our brains cease to receive blood, or sustain some very specific insults, memory probably remains a refuge even for the demented, who seem (in my experience) to dwell there as a place of comfort before they move to higher realms at their death.

The museum of my memory is full of images and artifacts wonderful to behold. There are probably snippets of every one of those 1200 dates. There are first kisses and first arguments. There are gifts and dinners that Jan and I shared. There are entire halls dedicated to events as simple as a walk on a winter evening with a meteor-streaking overhead. Other events of more complexity, like high school graduation, receive only small glass-covered displays. There are wings devoted to the first cries of our children as they were placed into their mother's arms and "under construction" signs for the halls of years yet to come.

At the ripe old age of 37, we pray that we will have many years to put into the displays. Our days and nights are full of things worth keeping. And unlike the computer on which I write, I don't need to hit the "save" button. Some things store naturally, like when the candle light of a restaurant glinted in my wife's eyes, shimmered in the diamond earrings and necklace that she wore so elegantly and transported me back in time at speeds unfathomable to physicists, but well known to men and women whose hearts are graced with great loves.

Breath Shepherd

I'm home tonight. Downstairs in the stillness of this house, my wife and children sleep in warm beds. Walking through the house at night is wonderful to me; a symphony of breath, each person a separate instrument as they collectively breathe in time to the metronome of life itself. It's interesting how something so common can move me so; but not surprising. How many years of my life have I devoted to breath? Or to its preservation? Airway, breathing, circulation; Always, breathing. And when I step, quietly, through the halls and doors of my darkened home, the rhythm of breathing fills me with secret joy and thanksgiving.

My wife Jan breathes heavily in her sleep, the breath of the tired laborer. Sixteen hours of parenting and the feather-bed receives her kindly, a worker who has earned her dreams. Sam, my seven-year-old, breathes like he walks, with stealth. A child who, with frightening silence, glides through the house and slips behind his victims to shout "gotcha!" He's my ninja. He loves the silence of the night, playing or watching movies, even driving in the car on trips. His breath is silent in the dark, as still as he.

Seth, age five, snores his exuberance. His adenoids are too large and consequently, his sleep is interrupted by sputters and pauses of varying lengths. His sonorous breath as disarming as his smile, as loud as the energy with which he approaches play. I worry about his breath sometimes, but not too much. One day, those adenoids need to come out. When he is in the right position, he sometimes breathes quietly, a stocky angel, smelling vaguely of brownie.

Elijah, age two, is so quiet in his sleep that I often stop and put my hand on him. His breath moves his chest only slightly and sometimes I am compelled to put my hand by his mouth and nose to be reassured by the warm, moist air that he softly exhales. Like his mother, he earns his sleep with intense play and more intense emotion through the long hours of light. Night is a relief for him and he crawls into bed with joy in his heart, asks to be covered in his soft blanket, and drifts away to dreams that I probably could not fathom.

Elysa, age one year, breathes in a whisper of air. To quote Doctor Seuss, "Like the soft, soft whisper of a butterfly". I can hear it but must listen closely. She is so bright and busy when she is awake, but in her sleep returns to the infancy so recently past. Sometimes I touch her too, and occasionally wake her by accident in my zeal to ensure that oxygen is passing as it should into her lungs and into the blood that rushes beneath her pink-tinged alabaster skin. Her breath, like a wee cup of tea, is sweet and warm and moves in tiny volumes.

It isn't always so lovely and gentle. I recall nights when respiratory viruses infected my children and when their breathing was rapid and shallow. Jan and I sat many nights by wheezing, struggling children as we gave breathing treatments and I wondered when to stop being their doctor, become their worried father and take them to the emergency department where my partners were working. The retraction of belly under ribs, the hollow cavity of the neck above the clavicles, these signs which we doctors fear in children not our own are harbingers of abject terror when they appear in our own and cause otherwise sleepy nights to be filled with hour to hour, minute to minute uncertainty. And then, what a relief when no tubes need to be inserted into tracheas, when no ventilators cycle to replace the normal bellows of soft breath. What joy when sick children sleep with no threat that they may stop breathing and parents' minds can slip away to peace again.

More horrible still, I can recall times when my children choked on food eaten too fast. I remember with anxiety the look on Seth's face when the air would not move, when breath was far away, crippled by the imperative airway which was blocked with food. I remember how we smacked his back, how his face turned from crimson back to pink and how thankful to God I was that he did not turn cyanotic and leave me. I remember my own times, waking with a stridor from some bizarre combination of laryngitis and overly reactive lungs. I know that horrible sense that air, breath, would never come again. Breath the lovely becomes breath the priceless when it stops.

Small wonder that the word spirit is derived from the Latin, spiritus, or breath. It seems, as our loved ones breathe, that life itself moves in and out of their bodies with perfect, cyclic regularity. As if every cycle reproduces God's leaning over Adam, mere clay, and blowing divinity and animation into his inanimate shape.

Certainly, as doctors we see the analogy. The math is so simple. Breath equals life. No breath equals death. Spirit equals life, no spirit equals death. And we therefore spend our careers watching the rise and fall of fifty thousand chests, listening to the character and quality of the spiritus that moves in and out of every patient for whom breath has become difficult, or in whom it may imminently cease.

So, there I am, a guardian of breath. I am night watchman for the lives that are part of me, my family who sleep within my hearing, within my touch and sight. It is my most sacred duty to keep their breath safe. But next, to keep the breath of all of those patients who are my own. Breath guard, spiritus shepherd. I roam the night with fear and wonder, watching, listening and feeling for anything that might stop the very thing that enlivens us all.

And so, I think I'll go back downstairs and get back to the work that I love best, and tip-toe between beds, listening, touching and watching as life itself floats through my family and my house for yet another night.

Dryer Guy

The dryer repairman came a while back, when we discovered that our clothes were still uncomfortably wet after spinning for several hours. This is why God made dryer repairmen. I've tried a few times to work on electrical things around my house. The desire to do this is somewhere on my Y chromosome. The voice that says, from antiquity, "You're a man, so look and see what the problem is, then fix it. Machines and electricity are your birth-right." However, the gene for the ability to fix things was completely deleted from my DNA. The last time I did it I was very nearly electrocuted under my house by a leaking water heater. A brief jolt of electricity and I was scurrying out to call a professional. Now I figure, repairmen don't treat their own heart attacks, so why should I fix my own appliances?

So, after an extended period of looking, tinkering, making noises and acting annoyed when I watched, dryer guy diagnosed the problem. Jan was home and I had gone upstairs to write or do something where I couldn't be exposed to AC current. He walked out into the kitchen and began to describe the problem to my demure, helpless wife. Then suddenly he stopped, looked squarely at her and said, "Could I talk to your husband?" I wish I had seen her expression. Doing a proper "about-face" she came to the stairs called me and said, "He wants to talk to you. Apparently I'm not smart enough to understand." I should have asked her to go and glare at some water to make ice. Brrr!

Seeing me, he began the explanation of things electrical and mechanical as if I had gone to dryer school myself. Nodding my head as men are taught to do to avoid appearing ignorant, I heard virtually nothing that I could have repeated. It was as if I had walked into an exam room where he lay bleeding and said, "Unfortunately, you incised the superficialis and profundis flexor tendons of your third digit. Fortunately, your digital nerve and

102

artery remain intact, however it will require orthopedic repair and local anesthesia. Comprende-vous?"

He did say I needed to go to Lowe's and find a replacement for the vent that blows the huge dust bunnies out onto the back deck. I can handle that. Satisfied that he had communicated with someone who understood the complex universe of large appliances, he left. I was grateful that I would now have dry towels. I turned to Jan and we laughed.

The point is my wife is really a lot smarter than I am. Sure, I know that medicine stuff. But by now, frankly, she could put on my scrubs and make a passable impression of me in the emergency room. Years of listening to medicine have taught her, well, medicine. Furthermore she is the brains of this entire operation. I simply need to explain this to people who call us about important things, like repairs, bills, loans or any other event or activity requiring a deep understanding of our home and finances.

Here's where it gets fun. We are about to build a house. Come January, large pieces of equipment, operated by very capable men and/or women, will begin to appear and be operated on the property where we plan to move. When that occurs, I am confident that the contractor, loan officer, electrician, concrete person, bulldozer driver, window salesman, well-digger and everyone else will attempt to speak to me in the erroneous belief that my wife sits in a corner, rocking and knitting, when not playing simple games with our children.

This will be a huge mistake. First, I don't like making decisions about things like this. She does. She has a vision of the house all the way down to where the outlets will go. All I know is I really want an air hockey table and a gun-safe in the basement.

Second, I make the money, I give it to her and she decides where it goes afterward. Any person seeking to receive due compensation for their labors will learn, early in the game, to go to my bride. I generally know if I have a twenty in my wallet to buy a sandwich on the way to work. Beyond that Jan's the gal to know.

So contractors and repairmen take note! My wife has the answers to the important questions. Don't ask me. Walk right past me to the pretty lady with the check- book. However if you're selling air-hockey tables or gun-safes come to me. And I mean it!

Betrothal

Romance, or the desire for romance, is a thing of titanic power. I remember the feeling as a child and teen; the urgency to be in love. The pheromone charged thrill of seeing all of the young girls in colored ribbons and later in red lipstick and high heels. The desire to be loved, the desire to love. The desire to desire. It was big medicine.

Looking back on the way that romance affects us all, I'm so thankful for my wife. I could have married some real (pardon the expression) wing nuts. So could she. We came along at the right time and in the right time were married. We weren't desperate, or enslaved to the idea of love. We just loved each other enough to navigate the equally treacherous waters of trouble and pleasure.

But now we have a new romantic fear to face. What about the children? Sure, they're little now. The oldest is only eight. But before long (sooner than I like, if I read the signs aright) all of them will be looking around at the opposite sex. And before I can swat Cupid with a ball bat, all four will be searching for love and passion. I know I'll be excited for them when they first fall in love. I know my heart will break when theirs do. And I'm sure that I will cry like a baby when each of them finds their true love and speaks their vows to God and man. But how do I get them there? How do I keep them safe in a world of crazies?

Talking to one of the other parents where my kids go to school, it became obvious. We agreed on a plan of attack. Betrothal. Sure, it sounds a little medieval. And it has been out of fashion for a while. But why not? Let the kids have their fun, meet new people, date, etc. But behind the scenes, mom and dad have arranged their marriage years before. We pick a family that has common beliefs and values, and a child whose personality seems to fit that of our own. We shake hands, sign papers and it's a done deal. And now, in an era of advanced technology and targeted marketing, we slowly begin to introduce the idea to the betrothed. We can't do like they did in the past, not to modern children. "Sam, next week is your wedding. You haven't met your wife, but trust me, she's a hard worker." No, these kids are just too suspicious. So they have to believe it was their idea!

I see "accidental" meetings on vacation. I see family outings for picnics and water skiing. I see subtle messages on websites and e-mails that contain the name of their intended, or that remind them of common interests. Then comes the tricky part. If they don't do it on their own, we introduce the idea. But with a twist. "Honey, I was talking to Sonya, you know, the girl we saw at Disney World last year? Well anyway, she's just not your type and if you even thought about going out with her, I'd forbid it. Do you hear? Forbid it! Her number is on caller ID. Do not call her!" That should seal the deal. A little more resistance, then a gradual acceptance and years of planning will come to fruition.

It isn't that I think my children are simpletons and won't have the capacity to choose a mate. I just find myself in terror of some of the people I meet in the world. I have actually considered sponsoring an emergency room waiting-area dating service. Because after midnight, there are some people who just shouldn't be in the general dating pool. Best to herd them together for the safety of the human species as a whole. Of course, even some of the nicest people I have met down the years have turned out to be the most bizarre.

So, in a suggestion full of stunning hypocrisy, I want to reintroduce the age-old concept of betrothal. Heck no, Jan and I weren't betrothed. But that, as they say, was different. The world is a now an exponentially more dangerous place. So I'll be on the lookout. My children are too precious to trust to the random chaos of the dating scene. Does anyone know three nice little girls and once nice boy?

Building

I'm watching our new house rise from the ground. Where there was a hilltop, overgrown with blackberries and mountain laurel, there stands a field. In the field, courses of logs lie atop one another. Large openings will contain glass windows that will look out across Cheohee Valley to the north. The roofline is notched like an enormous set of Lincoln Logs and soon a green metal roof will sit on top and play percussion in the falling rain.

In time the empty inside will take shape with walls and the nerves and veins of electrical wire, ducts and plumbing will grow along the walls and between the floors to give life to the awakening structure. Sinks and tubs, appliances and flooring, all the bones and joints will be formed and make it a thing almost alive.

I'm not a builder. Nor am I involved in the construction of my home except that I sometimes discuss it with the men who are building it. As one who can scarcely nail two boards together, I view construction with a wonder akin to space travel. I simply don't possess the skills necessary to build. I probably never will.

So I have a contractor and his crews to thank for the work that is making a structure of lasting quality for my family. I don't know how long the house will stand or how long we will live there. I don't know if my grandchildren will come there for the summer or if my friends will gather there for my funeral. I only know that I see its construction as a wonderful thing, taken too much for granted. The world in which we move is made and supported by the hard work of men and women of tremendous skill.

Our culture, swept away by technology, overlooks the things that it requires so much like breath. No matter how much time we spend in the sexy, virtual world of the Internet, our computers sit on desks made of wood or metal, usually fashioned by hand.

Those desks sit in houses or apartments whose walls of brick, wood or stone were also erected by humans.

The automobiles that carry us to professional jobs in clean buildings are produced in hot, loud factories by persons who actually understand the many wires that live in my vehicle. We drive on roads constructed by workers on giant pieces of machinery in the blowing dust and heavy mud of road-beds cut across places our ancestors would have thought impassable.

And as we work in our sheltered workplaces and drive our sterile cars, we eat food grown and harvested by people in open country, where the soil is like a currency and where nature can elevate or destroy a family in a season or two.

And if our food is served in restaurants, it is cooked over hot stoves and grills by people who breathe smoke and steam for hours to serve us meals that many of them couldn't afford. And it is served by other men and women who walk for miles in a shift taking orders and filling glasses so that articulate folks in professions, business and technology can look down their noses at waiters as they make the decisions on which the world so necessarily turns.

Or does it? As a physician, I'm a mechanic for humans. It's not that simple really, but pretty close. My work, all my effort, is to stave off the inevitable discomfort and final passing of every fragile human in my care. And while web-sites fascinate us, their virtual nature makes them anything but durable. How many million will be created, then disappear, in my life? As for business, sales and advertising, the things sold are often things that will pass away with the next fad, or the next trend in what America wants.

What do we want? We want permanence on some level. Sadly, our lives don't always provide it. So when I need to be reminded, I look at the house on the hill. And I think how long it will last thanks to strength and skill of laborers who work in the present, in reality, and accomplish things more permanent and more practical than most of us ever will.

Leaving Home (for good)

Outside, in the yard, lay the remains of summer. It was a good one, although too hot. But the children made the most of it. I can see a broken Tonka fire-truck, apparently not engineered for a 7-year-old rider. I can see the empty green pool/sandbox in the shape of a turtle. It has been a regular fixture for many years, a veteran for the South Carolina heat and cold. Near the end of the house, by the shrubbery is the yellow plastic gopher that cooled us by spraying water in a circle on well-cooked children. A few weeks ago I cleaned the 'Slip-n-slide'. It was new this year, but is already molded and worn, its tears partially repaired by silver duct tape. I doubt it will return next May.

The yard is a treasure-trove. For me it is anthropomorphic carnival of delights, as I attach significance to everything my wife and children have ever touched or loved. Our property is full of memories. I still find Matchbox cars, dog-chewed toy swords, dirty socks and rain-soaked, forgotten tennis shoes, with cartoon character logos, that were once prized possessions. Beneath the bushes lie cups that were filled with water or tea on hot days, and the driveway is the white and gray slate where chalk monsters appeared like cave drawings.

The entire place is the thing archaeological sites are made of. I think about that. Today's homes, today's everyday objects, will be antiquities in not so many hundred years – a short time given the span of this earth. So I wonder if those who ultimately sift through the remains of our lives will get any true glimpse of what I saw, or understand the importance of the things I touched, the life I so loved in my brief run on the earth.

It's more poignant now than before, because we are preparing to move to a new house. I find myself cataloging the contents of our house and yard, even the broken, dirty toys outside. I wonder what we'll leave behind. I wonder, in 2000 years, what will remain. Will our artifacts pass the test of time, as gold and silver did in the tombs of the pharaohs? It seems sad that of those ancient cultures, so little remains of the average person. But for us, maybe more will remain. Maybe if it's only the plastic toys.

We may do better. Technology may leave us the means to pass our pictures down for generations. It would be lovely if our families 20 generations hence could look back on us, and see faint resemblance in the eyes, the shape of the smile, and read our stories of the things we loved. It would be nice if they could confirm what I have always suspected, that who we are is lost only in name, and that our mannerisms, our passions, our tendencies and our loves as families pass on down the ages, if only in faint whispers and echoes of who we were.

But I cannot be sure what will remain. So I look across the yard and wonder. I walk through the house and touch the walls, and sit on the wooden floor. I remember the corner of our living room, by the heating vent, where Sam (then 2-years old) and I would play with a gray castle and knights on cold winter mornings. It was a holy place. Will someone understand that corner when they unearth our house in several millennia? Probably not. It will be decayed and collapsed. Memories can't sustain the physical world. They only enrich it while we live.

When we move, we'll leave the house where all of our children first came after they were born. In the halls, in the rooms, in the walls are our stories, impregnated emotions, memories of laughter and fear. In the yard, on the wind, in the earth we leave the laughter of summer, the happiness of our few, precious snowfalls. It will be a difficult transition for me, leaving our home to the years.

But maybe, sometime, a man or woman who loves their spouse and children will find a piece of our lives in the wood, in the dirt, and hear echoes of our time however faint and long past. Or if nothing else, they'll find a small, defiant toy that lingered just to remember us to a different time, and pass on a microscopic portion of the glory that our life together was.

Bookstores

I love bookstores. When time allows, I enjoy browsing in Max and Chelsea's bookstore in Seneca. It is just the right size for me. I am constantly interested by the variety there but not daunted by endless shelves of books that serve to further remind me of my ignorance. Large bookstores are wonderful but they intimidate me in the same way as the musty stacks of university libraries. But even the selection at Max and Chelsea's reminds me of what I consider to be one of the great tragedies of my life. That being, I will never live long enough to read, more importantly to know, all of the things that I desire.

Somehow one lifetime of some 70 to 90 years seems a short span. I think that 200 or 300 would seem more reasonable. But even that would likely result in frustration. Because one could read and attend school around the clock for centuries and still barely scratch the surface of the collected experience of humanity; still scarcely brush away the dust on top of the buried depths of human understanding.

We are allegedly living in the information age. We are daily inundated with it. Information races around us all day and night on the Internet. Computer programs are available that help us to not only learn more information but order and use that information to make ourselves, our families, and our businesses more efficient and productive. They are designed to lead us more solidly into the security and material success that seem to mark the ultimate end of modern man's earthly efforts.

Not long ago I read that no less than President Clinton wants to see to it that every citizen is using the Internet. This lofty goal may be a little misdirected, since it isn't absolutely certain that everyone wants to be online. But I'm sure it is a noble intention to give more people access to more information.

As I think about that word, information, I begin to wonder if it means the same thing as the word knowledge. My Oxford Desk Dictionary and Thesaurus indicates that they are much the same thing. Both use the other word among their definitions. But they have a different feel to me. Because I think that information has come to mean something that is goal directed and has as its end money, success or advancement, whereas the old standby knowledge is less glitzy, less sexy. It still sounds to me like classrooms with wooden floors, creaking desks and chalk on a blackboard. It continues to instill in me the sense I have when I walk in melancholy fascination down the aisles of a bookstore and read the titles, touch them as if to absorb their contents, then sigh to myself.

This is not to denigrate success or information. As a physician I need information as much as anyone. I need to know what's new in medicine, what's happening in government and thousands of other things. Information and its application, though I have somewhat falsely separated it from its sister knowledge, defines individuals, drives institutions and advances nations.

Knowledge and information are somehow unique personalities of the same entity. I was reminded of this recently by a close friend whose range of knowledge always astounds me. He assimilates and uses information with in an amazing way. He is analytical, logical and successful. Not long ago he looked at me and said, quite off hand, "I've been reading some Aristotle lately." He then proceeded to describe how wonderful his experience of this ancient author had been. I assure you, he doesn't need Aristotle to succeed in his profession or hobbies. But he desires to know as much as possible. It's reassuring to see how well knowledge and information dwell together in his outstanding mind.

As I look over the library that my wife and I have accumulated, I see books that touched me and still move me. I wonder how to make my children fall in love with knowledge as others made me passionate for it in years past. I want them to have access to information. But I want them to desire knowledge, to need it like air and water. If that happens, their education will be certain. Because, for all the modern classrooms, computers and money we apply, learning is about the passion for knowing.

The New House

When I finished my medical training, my wife and I moved to South Carolina and bought a house hidden in the middle of several acres of woods. It was cedar sided with cedar shingles on the roof. There was a fairy tale look to it. The yard bloomed every spring with azaleas, honeysuckle, mountain laurel, roses and dozens of flowers I couldn't identify in a hundred years. The front porch was a delight in summer and kept us from the intense heat of July and August. We worked in the yard, shielded by our pines and poplars from any view of the road nearby or the outside world in general. In autumn the trees blazed and leaves fell into our little, private valley. And the winter found us warming ourselves around a small fireplace in a living room built with dark wood on the floor and trim. It was safe and lovely just like a first home should be.

After a short time our children came. Four of them were born over a span of six years. Each of them came home to that house in the woods, three in winter's comfort, one in spring's warmth. They cried, nursed, laughed, crawled, coughed and had fevers in that house. One developed diabetes at age five while living there. The children referred to it later as "our baby house". For my wife and me it was a treasure vault of memories.

But as families grow larger, houses grow smaller. And in time we felt it was time to move on. Jan and I had purchased land and wanted a log house. Building it was frightening and challenging. But once it was finished, we knew it was right. Right, because from the back of our new house we can see miles and miles of mountains in the nearby national forest. Right because we are on a hilltop, adjacent to the wilderness that looks like our ancestral homes in West Virginia. We knew it was right because the wind always blows there. We knew we belonged because as clear as the stars were in our little valley, they're clearer here.

The move was not easy though. Moving is as much an emotional effort as physical. It has been harder on my three boys and me than on my more practical wife. The kids and I dragged and moped. As much as we loved the new place, we were attached. We were so nostalgic that my oldest boy, age eight years, said "I'm not sure how long it will take me to call the new house home". I didn't say it but feared the same. But now as we have finished cleaning out the old house and have fully moved into the new one, everyone is happy. Not because the new house and land is similar but because it is so different.

Moving has been a spiritual journey for me. And in the process of leaving one home for another God has opened my eyes to what moving can represent. More than the obvious blessings of simply having a home and land, moving has given me insight into our pilgrimage in life. Because what we are doing in this world as Christians is constantly moving toward a new home.

We aren't building it ourselves because we can't. But Jesus assured us that he was going to prepare a place for us. And I just can't help but see it as magnificent beyond words. His love for us finds analogy in this life in those who love us best.

Now this house, that I now call home, was designed by my wife for the comfort and pleasure of her husband and children. Even now I write from a loft designed as my office. She knew I needed a place to go to put words on paper. I can't imagine what Jesus has in mind for me in Heaven. I can't imagine what I need most that he is now preparing for the time when I arrive at his doorstep. But since I am so happy in this house of wood (designed by my wife), then my heavenly home (prepared by my heavenly Father), must be perfect. When I imagine it I can't see the house but I can see that around it rise the mountains of heaven. For if there are rivers and seas and cities, there must be high, snow- capped mountains and I hope my house looks upon those mountains and that snow.

But details and selfish desires aside, moving left me with another insight into our move to our heavenly home. Moving means leaving things behind, large and small. We have had to purge our home of stuff. And the purge is ongoing. But I am so attached to my memories, particularly those of my Jan and my little ones, that it's impossible for me to throw things away. I hold on to everything as long as I can. Even the bassinet, exercise chair, high chair and baby toys that no longer serve any function for my children are each precious to me. They're precious because my children touched them, sat in them, ate first bites of birthday cake in them. I could occupy pages with my profound attachment to the physical artifacts of my life. Charming as it is, sensitive as it sounds, it's a battle.

It's a battle because all of those things, all of those memories threaten to rob me of the joy of leaving an old home for a new one. At the same time they also threaten to rob me of the joy of looking forward to the next life when this one is over. The truth is all of our pictures, videos, keepsakes, drawings, certificates, toys, shoes, and everything else will go to dust. And our attachments to them, while sentimental and mostly harmless, can anchor us too firmly to the past, blinding us to both present and future happiness.

When we leave this life none of those things will go with us. It will all go either to someone else (for a while) or to the burning pile or trash heap. This is a painful truth, but a truth nonetheless. Fortunately, Christ gives us hope. In him we have a secure home in heaven, where we will have our loved ones, where we will have no pain or tears and where nothing we have will ever decay or be lost. "Where thief will not steal, nor moth or rust destroy." Our inheritance there is forever safe.

So in our living, it's helpful to think of our leaving. We leave a home on earth that can be such a pleasure, so full of comfort and delight. It's our baby house. But that's really all. Our house above is designed especially for us, with all of our needs and desires met. It's far away and the wind blows constantly. It is high as the stars but for all its terrible glory it's safe. And to get there we simply have to trust our builder, to lean on our Savior. And in the process we have to let go of the things that hold us here now. If we do we will be more than rewarded.

And our joy in our new home will be a thing worth singing about as the ages roll.

Cupid

It's time for cupid to disrupt the contented lives of men and women everywhere. Valentines' day is here to remind us that we all need a little romance. From heart shaped chocolate boxes to red roses, scarlet dresses to diamond rings, the fat little meddler wages an all out assault. But sometimes, especially for the single, the mad rush to establish relationships results in a little temporary insanity. And after the perfume and intimate dinners are gone, people look across the table at the person they most recently fell in love with and ask a simple question: "Who are you?" Because passion and loneliness frequently cause people to overlook the shortcomings and dangers of the men and women they want.

I was reminded of this while talking to a friend of mine about her children. A single mother of two little boys, she told me that her ex-husband recently struck one of the boys on the head several times. The child's head was bruised. I'm sure his heart was gashed. How do you bounce back when your father beats you? How does a mother deal with the fact that the man she loved, who fathered her sons, is so disturbed that he would attack them? I don't know. But I thank God that my wife is sane and good.

The unstable can be deceptive. They look and act like the rest of us in the beginning. Sometimes they're even more loving and devoted than average. Over time, however, their true natures become apparent. So it's a good idea to use caution, even if one of those little arrows hits you on February 14th.

It's difficult. I remember grade school and the delicious feeling that Valentine's day brought when hints of romance first stirred and manifested themselves in X's and O's on Bugs Bunny valentine cards and in the coy smile of pink-clad girls in pony tails. I remember the progression, as teenage years gave more substance to romance, when a kiss and embrace from my girlfriend set my head spinning. But one thing Valentine's Day never gave us was a sense of forethought. We never looked down the road past the delicious taste of romance.

I'm not a puritan or a cynic. I highly recommend romance. My first date with Jan was 19 years ago in January. We still celebrate it. Fortunately, through God's providence, we found each other and were both like-minded. Our relationship blossomed into a marriage of 13 years and four children. Looking back though, I see that I almost ended up with some bad matches. Jan would say the same.

I think that the desire for romance is so great in all of us that we sometimes accept it too soon. We hope that whatever defects we see in our loved one can be overcome "if we just love each other enough". I'm not so sure. Jan taught me to have fun and not spend my life in the library. She didn't have to teach me not to spend every night drunk.

People often "fall in love with falling in love." A special affliction of the young, they marry their first real romance or the first person who treats them as an adult. Their young identity becomes inseparable from the only person they have ever dated; their heart inextricable from the person with whom they first shared their body. But the pain of waiting for the best fit, the truest love, is far better than the false security of a tragic or merely tolerable relationship.

Everyone should be attentive to the behaviors of their loves. They should look for signs of violence or cruelty. They should look for indications that their loved ones will ignore them once they are committed. They should find mates of common belief and common dreams who will challenge them to go higher and further, rather than holding them too close to breathe. Parents should always remind children of their inestimable worth with or without romantic love.

Valentine's day is a heady time. It is a power that can make us all weak. But romance shouldn't leave us deaf, blind or stupid. If people pay attention they can often see the tendencies of lovers far before vows are exchanged or police officers summoned.

Cupid may enjoy starting romance but he doesn't have to wake up with the wrong person every day for the rest of his life. And no one else does either.

Human Voice

Recently my wife went to summer school. She already has a master's degree but wanted to take an undergraduate class for her own interest. It seemed easy enough. Go to local university, register, pay, go to class, voila! Hardly.

When she tried to register and pay in person the admissions persons were befuddled by her explanation that she had been "raising four children" in the interval since her last college attendance. Worse, they were shocked by her attempt to register in person. My wife, obviously the product of the medieval world, thought that she could actually interact with a human.

"You'll need to go to our website", the ladies at the desk said. So Jan came home and entered the new millennium of college admissions via the Web. It was possible, yet the process required numerous phone calls to confirm her registration. During most of these calls the person on the other end had no idea how to help her. Apparently, assistance and information were likewise available only on the web. (To Jan, this lack of human assistance was no surprise. She's still reeling from the tragic turn of national events that caused the untimely and complete extinction of gas station attendants).

I understand how colleges and universities would find it easier to use this method of registering already confused students. It accomplishes fairly easily what once required mountains of paper and lines of restless young humans only slightly shorter than queues for bread in Soviet Russia.

Still, I am concerned with the progressive separation of humans from humans. There are several examples in my own life. For instance, there's the annoying tendency of grocery stores to try and force me through the self-checkout line. I have been conditioned to do this by the fact that those lines are frequently unpopulated. But I usually approach the self-service line with a little anxiety. I always manage to do something that causes the machine to say, "ask for assistance". Or I fail to maneuver the dog food bag onto the carousel fast enough, and the machine complains, "please put the item in a bag". Furthermore, I love watching well-practiced checkout clerks ply their art. They know exactly where the bar code is on everything. It's like watching a professional athlete at work, swipe, beep, swipe, beep, without a hitch.

But this is small potatoes. In the progressive separation of human from human, two things are the worst of all. The first thing, the very embodiment of every sci-fi nightmare, the work of the devil himself, is the voice prompt. The second evil, the thing that John would surely have included in Revelations if he had known about it, is voice mail.

Whenever I call a business for a question, I learn that there are 300 options, all of which have recently changed to prevent me from memorizing them. Next, I discover that each option branches into no less than 25 other options. However none of the exponentially increasing possibilities answers the simple question I have. I might find "would you like to check your account balance in Japanese Yen?" but never "would you like to cancel your account?" Imagine how happy customers would be if the first option, always, was "would you like to speak to a human being?"

As for voice mail, I have tried on numerous occasions to call persons at the residency where I trained. There was a time when people with pulses answered the phone. Voice mail was only used when there was honestly no one to answer the phone. Now it is only one more way to screen calls, to defer humans from other humans. Since I love the sound of words, the sound of the human voice, I find this very disturbing. I also find it silly since I have many times called businesses, received voice mail menus and then been told on the tape, "your business is important to us, so please leave a message." If it were that important they would have answered the phone.

It isn't the minor annoyance of these things that concerns me. What concerns me is that one of our problems as a culture is a progressive loneliness. We live, work and entertain ourselves within very small circles, if not entirely alone. Maybe just a little more human contact in the day to day business we conduct would make us all a little more happy and a little more sane.

Bloody and Daisy

I have not been a child for quite some time. Even though my wife may disagree and even though my imagination is bizarre in its own ways, I have forgotten some of the delights of imagination. So, God sent my children to remind me.

All of my kids have had their moments. They have imbued teddy bears and other possessions with human qualities. We have searched for hours for lost action figures and have stumbled through the dark to try and find a missing 'cuddly toy' so that they would drift off to sleep. We have had fierce battles with unseen monsters and one another that have required me to simulate battles in our yard with sticks for swords. I have performed wild gesticulations against unseen dragons and slumped to the ground in movie quality imaginary deaths.

But my daughter, my number four, my princess has elevated imagination to a higher level. For her, imagination is nothing short of performance art. For example, last year she decided that she had me (whom she calls Papa), but also another man called 'daddy'. I tried to explain the problem to her:

Me: Elysa, I'm your only Papa. I'm your father. You don't have another one.
Her: I know. He's my daddy. He's in the war.
Me: No, sweetheart, I'm your daddy, I'm your father. See?
Her: No Papa, he's my daddy too. He'll be back.

I raised my eyebrows at Jan, Elysa's (apparently only) mother. She shrugged her shoulders and protested her innocence. 'I tried to explain that to your daughter, but she won't listen'. I finally realized the obvious benefit of the arrangement. I said 'Fine, your daddy can pay for your college education and your wedding.' It's hard not to get your feelings hurt by imagination.

But I enjoy her imaginary friends the most. Over the last year and a half, she has communed regularly with two of them. They inhabit her right and left index fingers like little puppets. Their names are Daisy and (get this) Bloody. You can see how I might wonder what medications are in store for my little fruitcake. Her brothers, who find it all most hysterical, simply prod her on. "Elysa, how's Bloody? Where's Daisy?" She's thrilled to have her visions confirmed by what she considers rational, responsible humans much older than herself.

So it was a sad day when we were driving along in the car and she told me, head held down, fingers up, 'Papa, Bloody's dying'. I decided to try and enter this world in order to bond with her tiny digital friends and their obviously terrible plight. 'What happened sweetie?' 'Bloody got bitten by a bear. He's going to God'. I thought perhaps I could suggest a solution. 'Should we take Bloody to the imaginary doctor?' Her answer was cold, calm and reflected her higher understanding of the laws of the unreal. 'No, I'll just imagine another one.' Here lies Bloody, age unknown, bitten to death by a phantom bear in the backseat of a Dodge Durango.

Fortunately, Bloody did not succumb to the near mortal wounds that his name prophesied. Elysa still communes with him regularly. But she has another friend now. And I think we're moving in the right direction because this friend is not entirely imaginary. My fairy princess introduced her new friend when she came in from the yard hoisting a twelve-inch piece of weathered wood over her shoulder and announced 'this is Loggy. He's my friend. I love him!' I didn't have the heart to tell her that he might be more appropriately called 'Pressure Treated Lumbery'. Loggy's name seemed so warm, so intimate.

She has more concern for Loggy than for others that have been citizens of her charming if bizarre private world. When it was recently raining torrents she asked, with tears, 'Momma, can

Loggy come in? It's raining and he's cold and afraid!' We both looked at her and explained that the porch and deck were veritable family reunions for Loggy and that it was unlikely that he would feel either scared or alone. (Even if the odds that he would be carried off and gnawed by a dog were fairly high).

Praise be, Loggy is still sitting quietly on the porch, unmolested by weather or canine. I'm anxious to see where the next inanimate friend will come from. The refrigerator? The recycling bin? The tool-drawer? I just can't predict. Because there's no limit to the adorable weirdness of a child.

I Knew Charlie Brown

There were Thanksgiving decorations in the halls of my children's school last week. They were handmade, cut and colored in the shapes of red, yellow and brown autumn leaves. We had the annual feast for kindergarteners, the boys and girls wearing un-naturally colored feathers and burlap buckskins (no one chose to be a pilgrim). Soon the halls will sparkle with Christmas tinsel and cutout green pine trees. The decorations awaken my memories of the smell of crayons, the taste of candy-corn, the voices of the children I grew up with. They speak to the child I remain.

Oddly enough all of the holiday joy at school reminds me of Charlie Brown and the characters who inhabited his world, to whom holidays were so special. Every year when the season silently pounces upon us I remember my old friends from Peanuts. I don't think of them just because they were funny or because of the nostalgia of lunch boxes and cartoon specials. I remember them because I lived part-time in their neighborhood.

Or I should say, I wanted to live there. They were my pals when no one was around to speak with. I could have navigated my way around their homes and recited the personal stories of each of the members of that little gang. The comic books where they lived lined my headboard as a child. I knew Schroeder and his passion for Beethoven. I knew Lucy and her 5-cent psychoanalysis (and her love for Schroeder). I understood Linus, his blanket a wall against fear, his insecurity balanced by deep spirituality.

And I went to school with Peppermint Patty; as I live and breathe, my classmate Melody T. was her spitting image, red hair, freckles and all. (Though Peppermint Patty would never have shocked my elementary school sensibilities by telling me to go to hell, which Melody did at the ripe old age of ten).

They seemed the perfect children to me. Not modern perfect. They were not the multi-lingual, over-committed, fashionably medicated, prep-school bound progeny of America's current frantic type-A parents. They were just kids like me. Sports were what they did for fun with no uniforms, no constant shuttling across town, no screaming, angry fathers or mothers threatening one another.

They lived in a world of bare yards and over-cast days, a world of gentility, where each one loved the others in deed more than word. They were never in a rush to grow up. Snowfall was still a wonder as the first flakes of the year landed on their tongues. Their stresses were small but real. And adults were just "wa-wa" voices in the background.

Learning was the duty they accepted without question (even though Sally always wanted her brother Charlie to do her homework for her). A kiss on the nose was scandalous. The little red-haired girl Charlie Brown adored was a mysterious, unseen delight. His unrequited passion was an echo of every boy's first wound at the hand of a little beauty. Love had nothing to do with sex. Faith was neither ignored nor pressured but natural as breath. Life moved at the pace of four panels a day, eight or more on Sunday, free of biting commentary.

They lived and moved in the place where children always should; between reality and fantasy; with the solid right angles of concrete daily life in constant tension with the Great Pumpkin, the wonder of Christmas and the bizarre actions of a beagle whose life was a blur of fact and fantasy.

I realize that when Charles Schultz was drawing Peanuts, the lives of children were far more complex those of his characters. Parents divorced and children died of cancer. Father's never returned from war. No matter how sweet the lives of my cartoon friends, real children were abused; real children were alone, just like now.

But my friends from that un-named neighborhood in that un-named American town represented an ideal. They represented a perfect dream of childhood and in a sense, of adulthood. In that ideal, I can be part of a circle of friends who will be forever ageless, accepting and faithful. I can return to that perfect world by simply reading a cartoon. Or by listening to the song 'Linus and Lucy,' that served as the recessional music when Jan and I were married. No matter when I go back, mid-summer, Thanksgiving or Christmas my old friends are still there and always will be. What a perfect holiday gift that is.

Cats Don't Hike

One bright summer day not so long ago, we assembled the children for a hike. My brother Steve was in town and wanted to go out into the wilderness with his niece and nephews. He loves the outdoors and works as a raft guide on the Nantahala River. The kids were thrilled. Backpacks were assembled with food and guidebooks. Water bottles were filled. Tiny pocket-knives were located so that the boys could feel armed and dangerous, elementary school Daniel Boones ready to face any crisis with their microscopic Swiss Army Knives. By the time we were finished it was mid-morning. Of course, in South Carolina mid-morning means "almost really hot". But we were undeterred. The woods around Tamassee were going to be our playground.

So off we went. We were some 75 yards from the front door when the tone of the adventure began to be evident. The adults were in the lead. Behind us were our older two boys, Sam and Seth, still ready for the day. Behind them, our two-year-old daughter was already screaming "Wait! Don't leave me!" This within full sight of her parents and her house. A few minutes more, almost off of our property, she began to stand at our feet, tugging at our shorts, hands extended upward, "Up! Uppy Up! Up mama, Up papa!" The hike would be more exercise than we imagined with some 35 pounds of toddler affixed to our hips, adding her body heat and sweat to our own.

Behind her, Elijah, age 4 began to remind us of the heat. "It's hot!" he said with a small child's unique ability to state the obvious. He wanted to be carried but was willing to walk a while, fearful of being outdone by his older brothers. Contests of machismo begin early in the life of a man.

But the visual that you need to really appreciate the adventure that day is the image of what followed behind the smaller children. Strung out in a line like mules in a pack train, were three 70 pound, out-of-shape, tongue lolling dogs and one panting, already overheated, 15-year-old black cat.

There was no running them off. They would not be left behind. Miserable, fly bothered, sun scorched, they followed us out the drive and down a nearby gravel road. Every so often one of the dogs would lie down and rest. Every 50 feet or so, with regularity, so did the cat, as if he were at the end of his ninth cat life, about to slip over the edge to cat heaven. His tiny pink tongue worked as fast as it could to cool him, but black fur just isn't practical in the southern summer.

So, about 400 yards into our hike we were carrying a daughter, fielding questions about "how much further" from the boys and to make things worse were attempting to stuff an old, grumpy, black cat into a backpack in such a manner as to keep his head out so that he could breathe and not get motion sick (which might cause him to vomit in the back pack). He hated it. We attempted to pour water onto the ground for him. He didn't get it. The dogs understood. They lapped up the water the best they could, wishing desperately that they hadn't eaten so much leftover pizza and had spent more time chasing helpless bunnies for exercise.

We finally made it to one of our destinations, where the air was cooler and the dogs found a large pool to splash in. But our pleasure was cut short when all three canines looked into the woods, bristled and began the low growl that makes astute humans say, "look at the time, let's go!"

We carried our two small children back toward home as the exhausted animals dragged themselves step by step back up the same road. Jan, Steve and the older boys continued their walk, even enjoying lunch in the woods. I, on the other hand, was on "grumpy child, dying animal" duty. We hoofed it home like wounded soldiers leaving the front. The children collapsed in the air conditioned living room and fell asleep. The critters drank water as fast as they could and vowed never to leave the yard again.

And I realized something. If my family had been the pioneers responsible for leading our clan to greener pastures in days gone by, we probably would have settled somewhere in the rugged, scenic wilderness of Manhattan.

Farmer Ed

Many of my ancestors were farmers and for generations grew what they ate. One was a vintner after the Revolutionary War. Between then and now they grew and tilled and worked so that they could survive. My grandparents continued the tradition and grew beans and corn, tomatoes, potatoes and squash until they became too ill to work. I hoed in the brown, creek-bottom dirt where we lived for my entire childhood and youth, following my dad's directions. Staking and running string, tilling and weeding. After storms I waded into mud up to my calf, barefoot, straightening bent stalks of corn. I have come to believe that this was probably a ruse to keep me occupied as I have never seen a large piece of equipment for Midwestern farm use called a 'corn straightener'. Still, it gave me many memories, strong muscles and an excellent sun-tan in contrast to my current indoor career and vampiric complexion. And it gave me a love of good dirt.

However I have few of my former skills these days. I did not inherit my family's facility at farming. I used my friend's tractor to disc my current garden and another friend's tiller to turn the dirt over and mix it. The tractor I sabotaged by not realizing that it took diesel fuel instead of gasoline. The tiller found me unacceptable to the extent that I pulled the starter cord at least 20 times whenever I used it, whereas my wife could start it in, say, 2 pulls. Last year's squash suffered terribly and the corn was practically still-born.

But despite these little set-backs I enjoy some things about gardening. Mainly I enjoy the fresh, rich dirt of spring. Its smell pulls me back to my home in a vivid way. As if I could look up and see my parents' home, white with green brick; and then up the road to see my grandparents' home, white wood beneath huge maples, all with cool, green lawns.

When I plow my garden I enjoy the sense of focus and separation. There's a meditation that comes with working in the earth however bad one may be at it. It lets me drift me into my own thoughts where I can rest in the realm of memory and hope, story and idea.

As I plowed and contemplated one day two years ago I realized that this ground of ours had, in all likelihood, never been cultivated. Of course, most of the world probably hasn't been. Still, it reminded me that there are still first things. There are still untouched places. There are still rocks that have never in all creation been held in human hands. As I tilled the ground and the smell rose up damp and dark for the first time, I felt like I was exploring something wondrous. I still feel it every time I turn over the soil and the thousands of bits of quartz it contains.

It's all the better when my children are running around the garden chasing each other, throwing dirt under the tines of the tractor, digging and exploring. They are new things, new life meshing with old life. Playing, they touch the memories the earth holds of beasts, flowers and trees; of native parents and children who probably played here, wondering what the ages held, never knowing my Elijah would find their beautiful quartz spear-point. And they drift through the spirits of settlers, with dreams of the land they walked across and what it could provide; of the houses and culture that grew up here.

It seems as if turning over the earth does more than allow vegetables to grow (and die prematurely). It lets the past nourish the present so that the future is more lush. And in our life we add to it. Someone, someday, will eat from the pear tree Elysa wanted or will find a toy or earring or other artifact of us left in the earth to educate the future about the passing of a bad gardener and his loves.

I am truly a non-farmer. But if nothing else, I can harvest meaning from this ground. And on its mixture of red clay, rocks and dark dirt, I can raise children who are connected to the land and the past even as they carry the future along. And if that's all I can grow here, then it's enough for me.

Gerbil Farm

The night of our anniversary my wife and I went on a short date. When we came home, my wife's sister Julie (who had been babysitting) met us at the door. In a calm voice she asked, "do you want to put the children to bed or do you want to catch gerbils?"

It became obvious that putting the children to bed would require catching the gerbils. Whenever the children were almost asleep, one of the newly escaped rodents would zip across the floor or dash under a dresser as the sleepy children watched. Each time, they were seized with the thrill of the hunt and jumped out of bed in pursuit of their six, free-range gerbils. Fortunately, small children, being fundamentally like small rodents, are very good at corralling hapless furry things. Since gerbil catching is not a solo activity, we all threw ourselves into the chase, children and adults alike.

I should probably give some background here. My wife's brother Dave and his wife Dawn gave two gerbils to our children for Christmas. Like good gerbil owners, they were confident of the sex of their gift. "I think they're both girls. Or boys. Probably." So, in short order, our fuzzy friends were expecting. And before you could say "prenatal care", we had four new, pink, peanut shaped gerbils. They grew up quickly, attaining gerbil adolescence in a few weeks. Then the trouble began.

You know the big, complex plastic houses for pet rodents that have exercise wheels, water dishes and tunnels for their occupants to explore for exercise? Well we had one of those, then bought another and connected them so that the growing family could have a little leg-room. However the adolescents, like teens everywhere, weren't satisfied. That was when the chewing began. All day, all night, one of them was somewhere trying to get through the plastic. I reconfigured, I taped, I looked at them threateningly. It didn't matter. One of them was always right side up or upside down in a tunnel, working his or her way through the walls of their plastic prison. It was like watching Steve McQueen in "The Great Escape". After a while I felt like the commandant of a stalag. So, when we went out of town one weekend, the gerbils made their break, probably planning to go to neutral Switzerland then on to Gerbil Land.

That brings us up to the chase. Two grown gerbils were loose (one of them again suspiciously overweight), as were their four offspring. Let me tell you something about teenage rodents. They're small, shifty and move at the speed of light. Over the course of an hour or two we moved toys, moved furniture, crawled on our hands and knees, yelled and laughed. My wife Jan, generally the very example of courage, actually lifted her skirt and said "eek" (or something like it) when one charged her with his little incisors at the ready. In the end, all six were once again safe in their plastic home and all four children were asleep with dreams of rats in their heads.

Did I say six? The very next day gerbil mom gave birth to seven more hairless bundles of joy. That brought us up to thirteen gerbils. Which I suppose qualifies as a gerbil farm. Living in rural Tamassee, South Carolina, I always imaged us with more, well, manly livestock. Horses or cattle, sheep or pigs, even Beagles. But, you play the hand you're dealt, I suppose. Gerbil farming isn't really lucrative, although there may be some sort of federal subsidy to encourage us to stop producing them. They aren't dangerous, unless you hit your head on something catching them. They don't get rabies or gerbil-pox. You don't need enormous rubber gloves to help them deliver their young. They don't require a back-hoe to bury when they pass on. And the truth is that the kids love them. All of my boys are expert gerbil wranglers by now. Even my daughter, petrified of bugs, thrusts her hand fearlessly into the mass of writhing fur to pull one out and pet it.

We've had good times, but some of them have to go now. The children are a little sad, but I'm expecting a new crop (or litter or gaggle) any day. Two now live in a kindergarten class, which leaves us with eleven. If you think you might pass our gerbil adoption screening process, let me know. I promise to give you two boys or two girls; probably.

Memories In The Heart

I remember Easter as the time when my Grandmother's daffodils came up. There was a long row of them alongside some enormous maples. My father and uncles had played there and so did I. Her complex yard with the garden plot next door made the perfect place for Easter egg hunts. In my memory I still see hen's eggs colored robin's egg blue and mint green, hidden in grass that had thrown off snow only one or two weeks before. I also remember eggs that were yellow, the color of marshmallow chicks, wedged in the crook of a low tree where my brother or cousins or I could easily reach them. I can hear the voices of my family and I remember how lunch tasted in Grandma's dining room. I could close my eyes and walk anywhere in her yard, anywhere in her house to this day these 30 odd years later.

The house belongs to someone else now but the memories still belong to me. They gain new life, though when my children ask, "Tell us about when you were a little boy," and I paint the pictures of my childhood in words for them at bedtime.

I have very few actual pictures of those times. Occasionally at my parents' house I will run across a box of disorganized photos with captions scribbled on the backs. Sometimes I see myself a baby-faced toddler in some checkered suit holding a stuffed animal, or standing by my parents, young and striking as they were.

I know that those pictures were taken to commemorate it all and strike a blow against time by allowing for something beautiful to be seen over and again. I hope that those photos stay in the family down the years until time dissolves the chemicals and paper, things as fragile as the persons they portray are mortal.

Now as husband and father, I take pictures and I have the added advantage of a video recorder to give me the wonderful combination of voices and images. (If only the other three senses could be recorded as well.) Like so many families, we have almost as many undeveloped pictures as developed ones. I watch our family life for perfect picture moments: all the children curled up asleep together; the boys mud-covered and playing with a water hose; Elysa in a pastel dress that she insisted on wearing and dared anyone to take off her. I look for reasons to take my wife's photo though she turns away like so many women, never thinking that she looks good enough when in truth she always does.

But sometimes I understand the real truth. And even as I take pictures and we squirrel them away into photo albums to pass down the generations. I know that it is almost an exercise in futility. I go to school events for my children or watch families on vacation and it seems that so many of them, of us, are obsessed with photos and footage. We watch our children grow up, watch our lovers grow older and we believe that images on tape, in albums or boxes will stave off the inevitable changes in our lives. That somehow these images will preserve the good and beautiful for us to revisit again and again. Sometimes we spend so much time taking the pictures that we miss the moment.

In truth our children will spend less time than we imagine looking back on pictures of their past. In truth, we will lose the pictures to fire and flood, or accidentally tape over a video. A century from now some of it will remain and some may end up on the walls of a sports bar that decorates with vintage pictures from the 21st century.

So it is the moment that matters. The ones we love, adult and child, will store the moments in their minds and imprint them on their hearts, as will we who observe. Better to lie down with the sleeping children so that they feel us holding them in their dreams. Better to kiss the lovely wife as she looks at the sea. Better to put down the camera and roll in the grass, jump on the trampoline and help the children find the eggs. Because the love we pour into the moment will find its way down the years to our descendants more surely than any picture ever did or ever will.

Follow Your Heart

My youngest boy, Elijah, who is 5, will have a kindergarten graduation this month, just like his brothers had. He'll walk down the aisle in a white cap and gown, sheepish and smiling, while we snap pictures and clap. And then, too soon, he'll graduate from high school and college.

He has plenty to do in the meantime. He needn't worry yet about how to spend his life, how to use his talents or where to go next. He's still ours. His job is to play and eat, wrestle and bounce, catch lizards, pet dogs and cats, and read books. His job is to follow his heart. And my job is to help him follow it.

If only we could explain that simple reality to every graduate and all of their families and guides. Because this time of year is full of speeches and encouragement, touching books and poignant bookmarks, and every sort of message imaginable to inspire young people to do great things and move the world by their contributions. But not enough people say what really needs to be said.

On steamy evenings, in crowded auditoriums across America, students at every level will be reminded of their duty to have high ethics and morals, of their duty to work hard for financial prosperity.

What needs to be said as graduates go out into the world is that duty, service and success are all well and good. But that their hearts' desires matter most. And if they follow their hearts' desires, good things will follow for all those they touch.

What needs to be said is that our lives are not simple, straight roads to a job, career, a spouse, two children, a mortgage, deep meaning, retirement, golf and death. Our lives, lived well, are pilgrimages through assorted pathways, where we frequently do not know the next step or the next resting place. And what needs to be said is that our passions and interests are keys and clues to our destinations.

If I've learned anything from my education and work, it is that who we become is often very far removed from who we set out to be or who we were told we should be. And looking back on my life, I see that our hearts' deep desires and final destinations sometimes begin to show themselves when we are only small children. Unfortunately, many dreams are destroyed early in the game because they do not look holy or prestigious enough.

Well-meaning parents and counselors can disrupt destinies with advice like, "You shouldn't be a comedian, you won't make enough money. Go into medicine!" "I am sure you might want to be a tank commander, but don't you want to be in full-time Christian service, spreading the Gospel?" "A jeweler? Why not be a teacher and help people learn?"

When we say things like this we may disrupt more than we can imagine. Because the comedian may bring joy to many (and might even make a living), the tank commander may witness to hundreds and preserve freedom around the world and the jeweler may do great things with her prosperity.

The best advice I have ever read came from Christian author Frederic Buechner, who said, "The place God calls you to is the place where your deep gladness and the world's deep hunger meet." The world's hunger meshed with your joy, your passion. What a remarkable insight! If I had known that, if I had understood that, I might not have done anything different. But I might have felt more free, more hopeful, more thrilled about responding to the many things that have given me "gladness" down the years.

As students graduate, we need to remember that they are unique creations. And that they, like we, are pieces of an enormously complex puzzle that extends from the beginning to the end of time. God made the puzzle and God knows what it will look like in the end. And we cannot predict, with either calculating economic precision or fervent desire for holiness, what anyone's place is in the greater structure. But in our hearts, God gives us hints.

And as these many graduates walk down the aisle, it would be well for us to stay out of their way and let them find their joy, and with it the path they were born to travel.

Kelly's Wedding

Our children were in a wedding recently. All four of them participated; three little boys in tuxedos, one little girl in white attempting to steal the show from the bride. It was an absolute comedy. Samuel, our oldest, wasn't quite tall enough to light the tapers assigned to him and had to be assisted by an adult groomsman. Seth, next in line, was ring-bearer but was more excited because in the tuxedo, he looked "like a spy". Elijah, next oldest, carried a basket of flowers for his baby sister, whose job it was to scatter rose petals like a little wedding fairy. She did her job wonderfully; but Elijah was petrified and walked down the aisle like a miniature (though well-dressed) Frankenstein, stiff and staring straight ahead, but unlike the monster, moving at a speed too great for effective flower scattering.

The ceremony began, but at the front of the church, Elysa was furious because she hadn't done her job properly and she intended, despite music and vows, to go back through the church casting bits of flower to and fro. Her brothers just wanted to sit down and stay out of the public eye.

As they sat, Sam leaned over to me with a program. "Papa, I want to be the ring beaver!" "Son, that says ring-bearer. Seth was the ring-bearer." "No, it says beaver. Ring beaver. I want to be the ring beaver!" (Two fingers held side-by-side next to his face, simulating beaver teeth). "Look, it says bearer, OK? It's just the way script is written. There isn't a ring beaver!" Muffled laughter from all boys, their mother and myself. My children are always ready to be the comic relief.

The bride was Kelly, our cherished baby-sitter. Kelly wanted the children in the wedding because they are like family to her and the feelings are entirely mutual. It was a delight to be involved in the beginning of her marriage. I'll always laugh when I think about the way the children looked and the things they said. But it was also a delight because it allowed the children to absorb the spirit of a wedding as it should be. And in an age in which we worry about the future of marriage for many reasons, this one was an object lesson.

I watch people closely. Partly because I'm a physician, partly because I'm a writer, I'm always looking at expressions and body language, always listening for tones and inflections, thinking about stories. And after I had finished watching my little princess and penguins, I watched the face of the bride. Chris, the groom, was turned away from me, so I can't speak for his expressions. I know that he loves Kelly, so I assume he looked about like men usually look under wedding conditions; happy face obscuring a kind of wonderful terror.

But her face, well it was the face of love. And her smile that day still defies any description. As she repeated her vows her eyes glistened, tears fell down her cheeks and she literally bounced up and down saying "I will, I will," her dress and veil rustling with the motion. When I saw that, I knew that she and her husband would be happy. A woman couldn't have that much joy unless she were secure in the love of her man.

I'm glad the children were there, because they watch things more closely than we ever know. And in the sanctuary of College Street Baptist Church, in Walhalla, South Carolina, a marriage got the best start possible with a host of witnesses, with family and with God. There in front of us was the essence of the salvation of marriage. Because without true, abiding love and commitment, without faith and promises, without delight and wonder, without friendship for life, no law, no constitutional amendment and no army of counselors will preserve marriage.

Replaying Kelly and Chris's wedding, I thought back to my own. I remember that after the ceremony, my friend and college classmate Sherrie said to me, "when I saw your eyes as Jan walked down the aisle, I knew you belonged together." Here we are four children and sixteen years later. You can tell a lot from a wedding, a lot from the faces in it. I hope my children got it all. I hope that they all cry and laugh when they speak their promises to their chosen before God and man. And I hope that in each of their weddings, there's at least one ring-beaver.

Puppy Obit

The puppies were born late last spring to a little stray we called Sophie. One day we heard them yipping in the woods and Jan found them under a laurel thicket, shaded by lush leaves, nestled in a cool depression in the dark ground. There were six puppies, brown and black, eyes barely open. Sophie didn't argue. She seemed pleased that we found them, though not as pleased as my three sons and one daughter, to whom gerbils became instantly passé. With excited children all around, we lifted the puppies from their hideout, put them into a box and let them live on the front porch, under the front porch and sometimes in our entry-way, where the cool tile was a restful place for the little dogs and their milk laden mother, panting in the summer heat.

They grew quickly. They were assigned names by Jan and the children. There was Luke, Rex, Trouble, Spot-Nose, Jack and Blackie. Their names, which had nothing to do with gender and little to do with physical description, shifted from time to time. One week Blackie had a black tale, another week Trouble had it. No matter, for they were all one pack, children and dogs alike. And the joy the children felt at having puppies was reflected back in the joy the puppies had in having children.

From the time we found them in the woods, the children coddled and petted the puppies. They helped the puppies find their mother's milk in the morning and evening. They held them in their laps like babies, or sat in rocking chairs on the porch, in the morning calm of the mountains and stroked their soft, puppy fur, as the dogs nuzzled the soft ears and necks of their children. I could always see one of my young, sitting beside a pup, hugging it, talking to it in the language of innocent things, which creatures and children speak with absolute fluency. These images burned into my mind as beautiful things do, the images we remember no matter how old or demented we become.

In time, we realized that we couldn't keep five adult dogs and six puppies. Some puppies needed new homes. Two found them, as did mother Sophie, though we nearly convinced ourselves to keep them all. Watching four children and eleven dogs run around in the yard was a little bit of Eden. Jan's parents live just down the road. Whenever I came home from work and saw their porch awash in dogs, I knew the kids were there. I also knew that the dogs wouldn't leave until the children did and that while the dogs were there, the children were safe. There was absolute devotion among them, regardless of species.

Two puppies remain with us, Rex and Luke, both females. Unfortunately, this Rex is actually Rex II. Rex I and Jack, the gold-brown twins, died. They became sick and the next day when had I planned to take them to the vet, they passed on, one underneath laurel similar to where they were born, the other in a dog house. I tend not to cry over pets, but I cried when I buried them together, as Jan did when she found one in the rain. The children accepted it all with grace, learning already as country children do that animals live and animals die. Elijah, though, still talks about the other Rex; they had a unique bond. That fact was the hardest of all for me. It reminded me that I can't shield my children from every loss, no matter how I try.

I suppose it was the memory of the whole thing, children and dogs together, that made me feel the urge to write what I see as an obituary to the two lost pups, a remembrance of a wonderful time. Dogs don't get obituaries very often, unless they're rich, or famous. Rex and Jack weren't rich. Except in love. They lived, in their less than one year of life, many of the things that everyone wants. They lived in a dog's paradise, with no leashes, no fences and no danger. They had tennis shoes to chew, a porch to lounge on, food and water and the company of kindred spirits, animal and human alike. Rex and Jack will be missed.

They are survived by their mother, their father (whoever and wherever he is) and by four canine siblings. They are also survived by four children in whose hearts they will always remain soft, fuzzy memories of a golden time. They were interred with a child's partially chewed sandal and a bit of blanket, at the end of the driveway by the porch, where the sounds of children and dogs will always be nearby.

Shopping for Gifts

I enjoy Christmas shopping. Buying for my wife and children is a special delight and challenge. As far as the kids are concerned I have learned not to buy toys just because I like them. I have purchased educational toys, learning games, brain development boxes and science paraphernalia for my children. What they really want (and these are from this year's list) is a truckload of topsoil, trading cards, Legos, Barbies for the girl, new Bibles, assorted weapons and various living creatures to fill the gerbil-void in our home. Things electronic (outside video games) fall flat at our house. So I'm learning to listen to the kids instead of my own inner child. (But we are not, I mean not, buying monkeys, snakes or groundhogs).

I don't have to buy for many men except my brother, dad and in-laws. It's not that hard really, except that we men don't do a good job of articulating what we want. Because when we do women (who usually buy for us) roll their eyes. "Well I can't pick something like that. You go buy it. Here's some money. I won't get the right one! (fill in chainsaw, shotgun, tree-stand, pressure-washer, golf-club, etc.) It's why there's that place in department stores at Christmas that has "gifts for men" like sock warmers, weather radios with attached tie racks and window scrapers with built in grill utensils. My advice to men is 'be specific, write down exactly what you want and prepare to enjoy your new pajamas.'

But the real problem for me, as for most men, isn't getting the right gift. It's buying the right one for a woman. Every man approaches this with a little fear. Young men buying presents for their first girlfriends struggle with it. (Minnie Mouse watch or real earrings?) Old men buying for their life-long partners fear it. (I can't remember what she wants!) All of us shudder a little when Christmas looms.

Think about it. If you buy your wife clothes that are too small, she'll think you want her to be smaller than her actual size. Therefore you have insulted her by ignoring the effects of childbirth and time. ("You probably want some petite model-type don't you?") If you buy her clothes that are too large you have suggested that she is fat and have, likewise, insulted her. ("What am I, a cow? Why don't you buy me a moo-moo! What do you want, some skinny girlfriend? Is that what you're saying?")

Clothes that are too conservative mean you think she is boring, that she isn't sexy, or is nothing more than wife and mother. Ditto with dull, flat shoes. But, four-inch platform heels made of clear plastic cry out 'hooker'. (Tip to men: don't buy shoes at all.)

Clothes that are provocative, like lingerie, sheer, low-cut blouses and mini-skirts can be acceptable in certain settings but if purchased without careful forethought might lead to this little exchange:

Woman: "Honey, don't you think this looks kind of slutty?"

Man: "Yes! Exactly! I knew you'd like it."

Purses are a nightmare. Men until recently didn't carry purses (and most still don't). We understood things like holsters, briefcases and wallets, but otherwise leather containers seemed all roughly the same. Watch a woman buy a purse. It's like some hellish scene from 'Goldilocks goes shopping.' This one's too large, that one too small. This one isn't right for autumn and that one doesn't have enough space for all the baby things. This one is only for summer and that one, well who would carry that color! Like shoes, men should steer clear of purses.

Jewelry is generally safe but wise men should avoid extremes. Like jewelry that looks too old (large brooches with fake rubies in the shape of house-cats) or that looks too young (like 'Hello Kitty' belly-button rings). Jewelry purchased from the Fredrick's of Hollywood catalog suggests that you ignored most of my advice, so you're on your own. Pearls, gold necklaces and bracelets, or diamonds (visible to the naked eye) might make up for the damage.

Things definitely not to buy women: sweeper attachments, power-tools, video compendiums of your favorite television shows (it wasn't her favorite, trust me), hub-caps, exercise gift-certificates, Weight-Watchers memberships, re-loading equipment, edged weapons, swim-suit calendars. Generally, anything you might want yourself.

So get out there and shop, my brothers! Face your fears! And take this column with you for reference. It might save you some explanations around the Christmas tree on December 25.

Leap Year

It must have been destiny. How, otherwise, would I have been at that Halloween party all those years ago in 1983, dressed like a doctor (of all things), while she was dressed like a mime? It must have been destiny that her friend fell in love with my friend and that our circles spun closer and closer, a new formed solar system of young planets, each with its own tug of gravity on all of the others. And it was destiny that her boyfriend was an utter Neanderthal, who treated her with disdain. And again that when we came back from winter break to study again, the snow fell so heavily that they canceled classes and we walked for miles, our little pack, to buy inner-tubes and slide down the white hills of a city park with all of the other students, wandering the streets free of classes and textbooks like liberated POW's.

I guess destiny had a hand when we slid down that hill and looked into one another's faces and almost kissed in the snow and later did kiss in the hallway of a dormitory. And destiny picked up steam from there and we were hurled down the years together through thick and thin, breakup and makeup, to here and now. I could tell you stories that would make you wonder how we stayed together and other, far better things that romance writers spend years trying to imagine, but which happened to us.

Looking back, of course, my marriage to Jan was inevitable. This is because of one simple fact, one hint from the cosmos that made it all obvious. What are the odds that a woman born on February 29, Leap year, would marry a man with the last name of Leap? I am reminded of our destinies because that odd, extra day is coming back this year.

I love my wife's birthday. It's one of those times when I can cause eyebrows to raise. On Leap year I can, in public, announce that I am in love with a child. "My wife is turning ten this year," I can say in restaurants. I can mention that "my child bride has four children already!" People who know us well simply smile and loudly attribute my statement to the fact that we are from West Virginia and we're probably cousins as well. People who don't know us wonder if they shouldn't contact the police or the Medical Board and report my behavior. I love their looks and then the smiles when I explain that it's all a trick of calendars, of extra seconds, minutes and days that humans add every four years to manipulate the oddity of time, which we so little understand.

But that's perfect. My Jan has never really accepted the existence of time anyway. When we first met, in the days of Halloween romance and snowfall passion, I was a serious student of the sciences. I rigidly protested that time had to exist, with little more logic than the existence of the watch I always wore. But she was firm, my timeless girl. "No, it doesn't. We invented it". It was that certainty, that ageless conviction (and the way she looked in high heels and short skirts) that sold me. And the more I age and resist time, the more I wish it away with the passing years of our sons and daughter, the more I read about the vagaries of modern physics, I think maybe she is right. Maybe we age only because our bodies deteriorate. Maybe time has nothing at all to do with it. Of course, I met my wife when she was not quite five years old and now, as I approach forty human years, she comes slowly upon ten. It's easy to be uncertain about time in our house.

So I have long since abandoned any attempt to understand it. I simply revel in the way that time swirls around us all and past my wife, who has a child's heart to accompany her single decade. I feel time tug at me but even our little ones seem to have something of her magic. In their faces and words, in their insights and questions, in their love of this world and their obvious citizenship in forever, I see their mother's influence.

This timelessness fills all of our lives with delight and hope. After all, at 80, I'll have a 20 year-old wife, who will doubtless look her age. Lucky me!

And I Pray

I am home in an empty house. My wife and four children are hundreds of miles away from me. The quiet is impressive, compared to the standard noise level, slightly less than a 747 on take-off. All things being relative, it's positively spooky without shouts and laughter, tears and protests, demands and endless, endless questions.

It always seems, in theory, so restful. When I am here alone I can sleep late and work or write without any interruption; for a while. But in the end, the absence of interruption is a problem itself. It makes a kind of abnormal sound, an echo of emptiness. It's a heartbeat skipped. So, I am anxious for the sounds and distractions to come back.

But it will be a while. And in the mean time we are separated by time and distance. And because I am who I am, this separation of time and distance is a source of anxiety for me. Separation from the ones I love most makes me nervous.

It helps that I live now, in this time of electronic signals. It helps that I can usually pick up the phone and within seconds hear my wife, and smile as the children struggle to understand me over the receiver, then argue about whose turn is next. It helps, but it isn't touch. I'm not there to help them if they have trouble. Voices, beamed over miles of earth and air, via microwave towers and through concrete can seem ghostly. The hug and kiss, the warm touch, is tangible and absolute.

So I wait for it. But in the interim, though I have the dubious comfort of technology, I have my prayers. Without prayer, I would be more fearful of any separation, since I know that life is dangerous. And because humans have always known this, humans have prayed for tens of thousands of years. We have prayed to whatever seemed powerful and capable of caring for us and giving us what we needed. We have prayed to wind and rain

159

and sun, we have prayed to trees and creatures, and to endlessly assorted gods. We have prayed for the mercy of the angry ones and the grace of the gentle ones. And now, in this modern country, in this rational age, we still pray for hope and help despite the doubts of many. We still pray despite the knowledge that we don't always get what we want.

I sound a little dramatic. After all, my family is in Ohio, not Antarctica. But consider how different life was before travel was fast, before voices and texts traveled at mind-boggling speed. Consider our ancestors who left continents behind, and in the process left families. Letters and news came rarely, and there was no way to share either joy or pain with the ones missed. Loved ones went to war or endured invasions, epidemics passed over like wildfires, marriages were celebrated, children born, parents died. The only thing possible was to hope and to pray. Hope is fine. But prayer was active. It implored infinite, omnipotent God to intervene for the good of those our forefathers couldn't comfort with touches of their own.

Even now, distance and time are barriers. We haven't yet learned to travel through them instantly. We haven't yet become the timeless creatures most of us hope to be. As I write this, and fret over a little trip, over a little time apart from my healthy, safe wife, sons and daughter, someone is on their knees, at home or in a dim church, mosque or synagogue praying for a son or daughter far away at war. Even now prayer is the only way we can surmount the distance with a touch, even if it is a surrogate touch from God.

It's a pity that so much of the discussion of faith in our culture settles into a dispute over morals and rules, over ethics and amendments, freedom and oppression. Because at the core of faith is prayer; whispered, shouted, screamed, sobbed, in the hope that benevolent God will reach down to this terrifying world and bring healing to the hurting, safety to the distant, peace to chaos.

And when darkness falls, whatever our struggle, whatever our fear, almost everyone wants to pray to someone. And that's where the truest faith begins.

Archeology

Much of my life has been a love affair with archeology. But perhaps I use the term too loosely. I have, indeed, been fascinated by history and the artifacts which bring it to us in visible, tangible forms. I am amazed at the idea that I can be in the presence of a thing, or touch an object, which was present hundreds or thousands of years ago, with persons long since passed away. The object itself is a sort of repository that transmits the echoes of human memory, human joy, pain and resourcefulness down the ages.

But while mummies, stone carvings, swords and such excite my imagination, my greatest love of archeology has lain squarely within the realm of my own life. As a child, I remember going through my grandparents' garages, attics and barns, and looking at things old and dusty. I recall rifling through musty closets and in long forgotten boxes for clues to the family I had been born into and for hints of their antiquity. It extended beyond my family, as well. I recall the hillside behind my grandparent's house on which a neighbor child had left a box of childhood treasures, bones of animals, gadgets and trinkets I can't recall. I knew vaguely where it was and would periodically navigate my way through dense brush to find the rusted lid, exactly where it had always been. I would open it and sit and look at the contents. Although the original owner was no longer there, sitting with a box of such wonders placed by another child was like having another child there. It connected me.

I suppose it is this intense fascination with such artifacts that makes me such an insufferable packrat. As my poor wife tries to purge our house of anything, I am found nearby, evaluating the potential flotsam and jetsam, looking and touching to see if it is of some value, not financially, but emotionally. I attach memory to things, far too often I suppose. I realize that even a house full to the roof of things is no replacement for the intense pleasure of memory, which can exist entirely in their absence. But somehow I'm addicted to the physical representations of those intangibles. And so it's an unusual thing for much to be discarded.

My wife and I have kept many mementos of our relationship, from inexpensive jewelry given on low budgets to pieces of paper with loving notes scribbled between classes over lunch. We have playbills from operas, posters from concerts, even a few dresses she wore to dances back when our love was the focus of two, not multiplied through the prism of parenthood.

But this behavior has reached its zenith in that rainbow. Our home is an archeological site in every room. The toy box in the hall is an outstanding example for I can go down through its layers and recall ages and events, times in which a particular toy was the grandest possession one of my children had ever owned. Times when that object was never more than a few paces away and accompanied the child to bed, in the car, to church and everywhere in between. Their clothes hold an intense memory for me, having held them, rocked them and played with them in those little bits of cloth. Shoes are the same. They hold something poignant, for they held something cherished.

I recall seeing a show on television about Hadrian's Wall, a Roman fortification in Northern Britain, and how the dwellings of legionnaires had been excavated. Families had lived with their soldier husbands and fathers, and among the artifacts was a pair of shoes, leather, about the size that a two year old might wear. I marveled that they remained intact, so far across the ages, and that they held the feet of a child like mine, loved by parents 2000 years ago the way we love our children today.

I am the archivist of my children's lives. I have kept everything including hair of their first haircuts, baby teeth, and umbilical stumps that fell off weeks after delivery. My wife and I store their drawings and pictures, write down their words, catalog photos of them and keep the toys that were too dear, too charged with memory, to discard.

I wonder why sometimes. Even if I could, in my old age, reconstruct my house as it was then and scatter the toys and games, socks, shirts and coats in joyful disarray like they are now, it would not allow me to transcend the demands of time. Time's passage is inexorable and its effect irreversible in this life. But somehow, the artifacts of my life still give me joy and will until I die. To touch the thing a loved one touched is not the same as their presence but it is, when combined with memory, a marvelous stimulus to the intensity of memory.

Even though I am the archivist, there may one day be an actual archeologist studying what remains of us. I want her or him to look at the artifacts of our lives, broken down items, crumpled pictures, clothes of children preserved by boxes but worn by time, and see one thing. I want them to see love. That we loved our existence, that we loved our lives with an intensity that defies time and that makes death the irrelevance that it ultimately is. I want them to know how wonderful my wife was, how elegant in bearing, how lovely in pregnancy. I want them to know how beautiful and strong were my sons and daughter, and to know their names and write articles or stories or poems to these characters from antiquity.

And if that occurs and they come away stirred with passion for the loves of their own and if they are imprinted by our names, or our faces, or the treasures of our lives, then we will have not only showed the wonder of our lives, but passed it, and ourselves, forward to another time.

Beach Exodus

This is our reading, from the book of Vacations, Chapter 10:

Once, to honor the birth of a small angel in our home, we traveled to the far away land called Myrtle Beach. We left in the darkness, while all of the angels slept. And we arrived in the darkness, and led the angels from the SUV into the inn. And during our time there we prospered and were welcomed by smiling persons in restaurants and theaters who greeted us with open hands, into which we dropped money and credit cards. And the angels lay on the beach and swam in the pool happily.

But after a while we had sojourned too long at the land of the beach. The merchants and innkeepers there had deprived us of too much of our money. We had lain too long in the lazy river beside the inn and had built enough castles of sand. And there were plagues. We were beset by the plague of sun, after which our skin was red, sore and most itchy. We were beset by the plague of sand, which verily did find its way into every body crevice, and into every piece of our luggage. And we were cursed by the plague of sleeplessness, which was delivered at the hands of the four angels who kept us up late, then woke us too early each day demanding sacrifices of Pop-Tarts and doughnuts.

And having been plagued and impoverished thus, we woke and said, "Let us get out of here, for in our own home, though there be no ocean, there is food other than French fries, there is room to relax and empty the sand from our clothing, and there are doors with locks which the small angels cannot open." And so our exodus began, and then we did pack the SUV with every manner of clothing, damp towel, beach toy, seashell and action figure.

Lastly, therein we packed the four angels and prayed that God would make them sleep. "Please God" we prayed thus, "let them sleep awhile that we may hear ourselves think". And God listened to our prayer, and ignored it, and gave the angels energy and to spare. And they talked endlessly and loudly about bizarre and confusing things, about visions and one another, and touched each other painfully and too often. They asked far too many questions, and for a few hundred miles were fascinated with water towers. They also made odd noises that mortal adults cannot comprehend. But still we drove into the West, to the promised land of Tamassee that we call home.

Yet along the way, another plague came upon us, which was the plague of the bathroom. And when the four angels were not discussing crass things, or playing eternal games of "I Spy", they were screaming about their need for the bathroom. So we did stop, sometimes four separate times for four separate angelic bladders in one short hour. And thus our progress was slow, and the great hot expanse of South Carolina still stretched before us. Sunburned, sandblasted and irritable, we continued.

But God guided us, and showered us along the way with chicken nuggets and soda, so that we did not faint from hunger or thirst. And he gave my wife peace, so that she drifted into the trance called a "novel" and heard little of the four angels, being swept up in visions of her own. Along the way the four angels chanted to their idol, called "the Happy Meal", and though our SUV overflowed with small plastic objects from these meals, we purchased them anyway, so as to occupy the four angels while our journey continued.

We were most tired, and we became trapped awhile in the village of Columbia, in the oasis they call Columbiana Mall. There we ate and walked, in hopes that large blood clots would not form in our legs. The angels played and went to the bathroom, and ate food over and over again. And God said to us, "Go on home, crazy people!" But not before he again empowered our angels with caffeine, and made their bladders shrink. Then, when we had traveled across the state for twice as long as it should take, passing the cities of Greenville and Clemson, we pulled into our drive. And the angels were tucked into bed without violence. And before falling asleep, we praised God for our deliverance, from beach, from angels and from the long exodus of the highway.

Morality

When my children are teenagers, and they feel the need to be with the opposite sex, what should I tell them? When they find a first love and want to give themselves away without understanding why, what shall I say? When they grow a little older and the gift they want to give to their love is the gift of touch and passion, what advice will I give?

Conventional wisdom would suggest that I tell them the mechanics of it all and then warn them about unwanted pregnancy and sexually transmitted diseases. That I explain to them that they are feeling natural urges and that those urges, if exercised with appropriate technical caution, are perfectly fine. But then, maybe modern wisdom isn't so wise.

Statistics on STD's, at least in South Carolina, suggest that technical precautions aren't doing so well after all. In spite of widespread public education efforts, in spite of an enlightened, more cosmopolitan view of sexuality, people are still having natural, unprotected sex with persons for whom they feel natural urges. And HIV and other naturally existing organisms seem to be benefiting nicely from the arrangement. Death, also natural, seems to be the result for far too many.

HIV is a horrible disease. It is robbing people around the world of years of life, love and joy. It is wrong to stand in cruel condemnation over those who suffer from this disease. They are being punished daily by the tiny virus that now rules their lives and holds their destinies hostage.

However we need weapons against this disease. Two of the most powerful pieces of the arsenal are politically incorrect. First is accountability. It is a rare person who has not heard of the predations of HIV. Most people know that it is spread by unprotected intercourse, especially with strangers and multiple partners. Most people know that sharing needles during IV drug abuse also spreads the disease. Those who continue to engage in these activities should not express surprise when they become infected. They should not pronounce blame on the government, economic inequality, pharmaceutical industry lassitude, racism, sexism, homophobia or anything else for their situation. If they were informed (and most persons now are), then they ignored risks and are accountable for their own behavior.

The other unpopular weapon we can level against HIV is morality. We'll be talking about that a lot at our house as the kids grow up. But not because I want to oppress them, make sexuality dirty, turn them into neo-puritans or stamp all of the fun out of their otherwise joyous lives. Quite the contrary, morality liberates. And that's what I want to tell them when they grow into the amazing adults I know they'll be.

I want to tell them that sexuality is God-given. It is one of life's great wonders and mysteries. And it should be explored vigorously within the bonds of their marriage, wherein it is not (hopefully) subject to uncertainty, insecurity or fear of rejection. It should be experienced within the safety of that bond, where disease has no opportunity to disrupt their lives with pain, infertility or death. It should be a delight they know without sneaking behind the backs of jealous spouses, or angry, hurt ex-lovers. And it should occur in marriage so that, should a child be conceived, it can be anticipated and received with joy, expected or not.

Sometimes the truth is hard and the mass of men and women aren't really interested in it. Like this truth: God built some immutable laws into this universe. Some are physical. Don't jump out of an airplane without a parachute. It might be fun for a while but the ground will come up faster than you think. Some of those laws, however, are moral. If we could ignore a little of what we learn from movies and television, if we could realize that screenwriters and social scientists don't always have our best interests in mind, we would see that the Judeo-Christian tradition sets forth some laws about morality, in this case sexuality, that are reasonable and good.

Those laws exist to give men and women lives free of pain and danger and full of pleasure within a few simple confines. And as the HIV statistics suggest, we ignore those laws to our peril. But since it may sound hypocritical, given the fact that we all have made errors in judgment and morality, maybe I should say that we ignore these laws to the peril of our children. What could be a greater motivation than that?

What Were You Thinking?

'What were you thinking?' It's a question I have been asked on more than one occasion in my life. It's usually a question that women ask men. And it is clear that frequently, the honest answer is, 'nothing'.

We tend to do things without thinking at all. Like the time I asked my ex-girlfriend of 4 years to borrow her ski bibs so I could take my new girlfriend (now wife) on a ski trip. If looks could kill...

This tendency to the impetuous also explains the fact that young men have lots of accidents, from car wrecks to ankle fractures, gunshot wounds to snake-bites. When we are young, it sounds interesting when someone says, 'Dude, you know what would be cool? Let's put some bottle rockets in a gallon of gasoline! You go first!' When we are young, it seems rational to attack a 320-pound linebacker because he looked at your girlfriend in a lurid manner and questioned your manhood. Thanks be to God and the overworked angels, most of us make it to adulthood, even though we weren't usually 'thinking'. But I'm afraid it doesn't end there.

'What were you thinking?' may be one of the most common expressions heard in married households. I remember when I had been married less than one year and heard it. I was in my residency training and also in the Air National Guard, and I signed up to go to a training course for two weeks. I didn't tell my wife, probably because I would be gone on her birthday. So there we were at a Valentine's Day ball (a mere week before my scheduled trip) when one of my instructors asked, 'So, you ready to go to Texas?' I don't know when I intended to tell Jan. Perhaps as I walked out the door, suitcase and uniform in hand. But she gave me the look that says it all. The look that every husband, when he is young and stupid, receives from an intelligent, vibrant wife. The look that said, 'What were you thinking?'

It has happened many times since. 'What were you thinking, letting the boys play with a hatchet?' Point well taken. Stitches resulted. 'What were you thinking when we needed money for moving and you spent $300 at a gun-shop?' Also well spoken. Besides, a .357 Magnum with a 2-inch barrel just isn't any fun to shoot. I sold it. 'What were you thinking when you signed up for high speed Internet that didn't work, then forgot to cancel it for 6 months?' I don't know honey. I just don't know.

Now, I'm not in any way complaining about my dear wife. In fact, I applaud her. She is always lucid and clear-thinking. Every time she has asked me 'what were you thinking?' it has been a reasonable question, to which my answer was always, in retrospect, silly.

Which brings us to the most recent episode. My daughter is learning to write her letters. I have a calligraphy set with a glass pen and a bottle of ink. Elysa loves this pen, loves the ink, loves the elegance of it. Once she used it, with me nearby, and did great. A few days ago, however, I left her alone on the kitchen counter with the same equipment and a few sheets of paper.

She came to us in our room and said, with a contorted and frightened face, 'Papa, I had an accident with the ink'. I felt my throat tighten and my heart race; my chest seemed to have all of the air sucked out. 'I'm coming sweetheart'. I rushed downstairs to find what looked like, well, here are a few metaphors: 'the brutal murder of an octopus', 'the explosion of an ink grenade', 'a bottle of midnight sky poured on the floor'. What it was, in harsher terms, was almost an entire bottle of deep Indigo ink, slowly soaking its way into our hardwood dining room floor. I dropped to the ground with a towel in hand, as Elysa tried in vain to remove it from her own body. I wanted to say, 'Girl, before you clean your skin, help me clean this up so we can save our skin!' I went through two huge towels, spread ink to places it hadn't yet reached, and turned my own hands the color of Papa Smurf before it looked... like a hardwood floor with a blue wash across it.

I knew my wife was annoyed, but she's a patient woman. She didn't yell at either of us. I thought the new color scheme was kind of avant-garde. Later, her eyes asked me the salient question. You know it. 'What were you thinking, giving a four-year-old child a bottle of ink?'

Nothing dear, nothing at all. Have I told you lately how much I love you?

Elijah Shifts Gears

I remember the way it felt to ride in my dad's truck. It was a used Ford F-150. It was a color that resembled purple, but wasn't really any identifiable shade. When I rode in it with my dad, I felt like I was a man. Whether we were picking up a tiller, or driving into the country to buy some goats, I felt a sense of initiation. When I road in the bed (gasp), like most boys did back then, I believed that I was flying, and I looked over the side as the gravel and asphalt raced beneath, tiny cities to my bomber high in the clouds.

We have a little 'farm truck' now. It belongs to our extended family. A collective truck, as it were, like we were good Soviets. I don't even know who made it. Like my dad's purple truck, it's a sort of indistinct gray, punctuated by red rust. The steering column moves at least 5 inches up and down, and not long ago, the power steering died, and driving it was like pulling an angry horse through a dog show. It just wouldn't go.

This truck serves a few functions, but one of the most vital is to ferry our garbage to the 'convenience' centers scattered around our county. We live too far out to have trash pickup. We used to have big green dumpsters everywhere, so that the drive to the dumpster was a matter of minutes. We used the dumpsters as navigation points. "We hope you can come to our Christmas party. Take Highway 183 until you see the green dumpsters next to Highway 11. For scenic interest, you may see bears in those particular dumpsters." It's true. Even the bears liked the dumpsters.

But alas, the dumpsters are no more. And we have the truck. We load everything in it, and then roll the dice to see if the convenience center staff will allow us to leave our offerings to the gods of the landfill. Household garbage, old televisions, mattresses, dry paint cans, most of it is just fine. I suspect that a properly wrapped human corpse would get very little attention, so long as your recyclable plastic bottles had the lids removed. So you can see, trash day is a big event.

My children love to go on trash runs. The truck is little, so I usually take only one child. Elijah, who is six, gets a huge kick out of going, and also works hard when he accompanies me. He's thin but tall for his age. And he has an old soul. Any opportunity for a little adventure and he's there. A few days ago I went on a trash run with Elijah by my side. Now, technically, he's a little too small for the front seat. But I'm a bad doctor (though a fun father), and my children do things that would cause the American Academy of Pediatrics to go into a cold sweat and swoon. (Trampolines, archery, BB guns, that sort of stuff). So Elijah sat 'shotgun' by my side.

The truck is a five speed and as I pulled out of our gravel drive, he asked me how the gears work. He's a little scientist and always puzzles over everything. So I put his hand on the gear-shift that sticks up from the floor-board. And I put my hand on top. And as we drove, I showed him how each gear felt. I made him listen to the sound of the engine as it was time to shift. And after about 10 minutes, I let him shift on his own. You know, I think he got it! If his legs were long enough, I'd have to hide the keys. He smiled his subtle, understated smile. His 'I understand' smile, and he filed the information away along with his data on black holes, the speed of light, rockets, nuclear munitions, swords, human anatomy and automatic weapons. We continued on our trash run, and I felt that much closer to my youngest boy.

I was reminded that day of how much of my children's learning comes in small doses, day by day. In an age of 'quality time', in an age of classes and camps and private schools, in a profession that could easily take me away from them, I see how desperately they need for me to talk with them every day. They desire, also desperately, for me to teach them.

I have unique gifts to give my children, born out of my experiences and knowledge. These are the things our children cherish, the things they brag about to their peers. These are the things that help identify them as special parts of a special family. I can teach my children some medicine, so that one day, on a camping trip with friends, maybe they'll know what to do when someone gets hurt. I can teach my children the power and importance of faith. I can extol them to love words, so that they can enjoy books and write their thoughts clearly. I can't teach them how to work on cars, since I don't know how. But I can teach them how to drive well and safely. I can teach them a few things about nature, and about how to shoot; how to exercise and how to create the perfect sarcastic remark. These are the things I have for them. They were born to their mother and me. I can only give them what I have. So my gifts to them must be their destiny, must be somehow a part of what they will need in this life.

In the process, of course, they teach me. They teach me about perspective, about wonder, about fear, about the importance of affection. They teach me the magic of life in the creatures they catch; they make me ask important questions when they say things like, "will you die someday?" My children teach me how to play, a lesson I need over and over. They remind me daily of the power and relevance of imagination. They teach me about my own inability to survive any combat game they play on the X-Box.

The subtext to all of that teaching and talking is a chance for me to teach them about even deeper things. When we talk, we often end up on living and dying. We discuss love and anger, hope and prayer, God and Heaven, hell and the devil. We talk about one another, and our futures together and apart, about wives and spouses, about the children they will one day have, and the dreams I have for their lives. When we talk, we know and love one another more deeply.

Medicine isn't important enough to take me from my children. I have a duty to them. Generations of children have suffered from the professionalism and success of their parents. When all they really want had nothing to do with money, clothes, cars or toys. What they really want is some equivalent of a worn out truck and a trip down a gravel road, with their hands on the gear-shift and their parents' voices filling their minds and hearts with knowledge and love.

The Between Time

This is the between time in these Southern mountains. The nights are cold, but not too cold. The days are warm, but not too warm. The landscape changes a bit at a time. Flowers and buds slip out, scouting the land, fearful of frost but unable to hold back any longer. Birds and insects are increasing in number. I believe a grouse has made its nest near my drive, and flushes whenever I drive past. On warm winter evenings I'll sometimes hear frogs, tempted by the temperature.

The steep ridges are still stoic, leafless, sitting with their backs to the prevailing winds; giants meditating cross-legged as they have since creation. We have seen snow blow over them, and rain, and watched the abstract art of clouds swirl above their bare trees, bringing us shapes of dogs and dragons, cats and castles. But even those mountains will change and put on new clothes, will seem alive when dogwoods, rhododendron, laurel and all the rest dress them with the power of their cyclic loveliness. Like a wife to a husband, saying 'get up and get dressed, we're going out!'

All this change is common; eons common. In my short 40 years I've seen it over and over. I know what to expect. By now, though I love fall and winter most, I'm already anxious for the easy winds of summer, for days at the lake, for long weeks enjoying the children at home. I look forward to a lavish time, without homework or schedules to disrupt the casual pleasures of our life.

The children are changing like the mountains and all that lives upon them. And that is something I'm only just learning to accept; something I resist like I resisted melting snow when I was young. Each child is a landscape. And each of them is in a unique season. My wife and I study the weather of their lives, watch as they rise higher, and the sun and storms move across their faces and bodies. They are worlds of their own.

Like the spring mountains under which they are growing, each is decorated with beauty. There is the unruly, flying blonde hair of our daughter like wild grasses in the wind; there are the deep, pleasant valleys that dimples form on the faces of my sons. And there are the strong arms and legs of each child like the young River Birch in our yard, soft and pliable for now; one day rock solid like our rare Oaks, prepared for anything. They have depth in their eyes, two with brown eyes and two children with blue. The ages are reflected there and there is such beauty that it looks like the spring sky and the autumn earth inhabit their irises as they look into mine.

As the weather warms they'll be like little mountain animals thrilled with spring. The youngest a little fox kitten, a work of art, dancing to unheard music, poking her nose into everything. The next, my youngest boy, a curious raccoon, his long fingers touching and manipulating and discovering whatever he sees. The next boy a young bear, strong and anxious to prove it. He doesn't realize how might and gentility fuse in him. And my oldest son, a young buck deer, fleet, alert, not quite ready to fight, but feeling it, smelling his destiny in the air, itching for the challenge of adulthood.

In the shadow of this log house, in the shadow of the mountains, with nature all around, their seasons are turning. I've seen winter turn to spring. But I have never watched my own children grow to adulthood; a change that is more climactic than seasonal, and which alters their lives, and ours as their parents, permanently.

I don't always like it; I resist it with that old, tired futility. But it is the way of things, and not for me to like. Nostalgia for childhood is a delight, but also a luxury. Life is so precarious that it's a great blessing that my children are growing older; a gift that the natural histories of their lives move ever forward, wrapped in the trees and leaves, winds and mountains of our home.

So I'm thankful, and I pray that my little creatures will see their own young one day. I pray that they will revel and delight in their own children's changes. And I hope that they learn to love each season, of earth and humanity, in all its variety. Just as I am learning now.

Dance to be Alive

This past March our family traveled to Indianapolis, where I was speaking at a conference. One evening Jan and I wanted some curry, so we went to an Indian restaurant near where we once lived. It was peaceful inside, with a cold Mid-Western wind blowing snow flurries across the parking lot. Indian music played over the stereo, with sitar, drums and other instruments that sounded like a distant place and time. While we looked over the menu, an amazing thing happened. Our four-year-old daughter Elysa was possessed by the spirit of a belly dancer.

Anyone who knows her understands that Elysa commands attention. But this was different. Wearing her sleek black velvet pants and blouse, she looked a little like a blonde-headed panther. She began to shimmy and shake, holding her hands over her head, rolling her hips in a circle that would have dislocated the joints of normal adults. She twisted and turned, looking over her shoulder, blue eyes beaming, smiling as only she can. She rolled her wrists to the music, stomped her feet to the Asian tempo. Finger cymbals and a coin belt are the only things that could have completed the visual effect. Waiters paused to watch her and said, in thick accents, "you love to dance, don't you, little girl? " Her mother and I just watched in amazement. If there had been other patrons nearby, I'm sure they would have thrown money. Looking back, I think we could have gotten at least an order of Chicken Tandoori for her performance, but I was too stunned to ask.

Eventually, she became a little girl once more, and settled down to negotiating about how much she had to eat. But I'm sure the muse will visit her again. Probably about the time she is a freshman in college; right about the time my hair explodes in gray. But it's all good. Elysa was born to dance. It is as natural to her as breath, a perfect expression of her love of life.

She has wanted to dance since she knew what the word meant. Her favorite question to me, at age 2 or 3, was "Papa, do princesses dance?" Obviously, she was trying to reconcile her two personas; princess and dancer. So, it was with much joy that she began her first dance class last fall. She wasn't there for the outfits, though she will play and sleep in leotards whenever she can. She wasn't there for the social interaction. She was there to dance. And she has loved every minute for the last 10 months.

Never before having a daughter, and never having been a girl, I didn't understand this 'dance thing.' But now as a father, now having watched my own child and dozens of others in her school, I'm getting the picture. And the picture became exceptionally clear over the past weekend at the yearly recital that the 'Dance Discovery' dancers gave at the Brooks Center, a performing arts center in Clemson.

There I saw what it was that possessed my daughter. It was a celebration, for both female and male dancers. It was the joy of movement, the delight of music, the love of elegance, the wonder of the human form. Whatever the age of the dancers, I saw them on the stage, fully alive. Young men exhibiting their fitness and strength, their delight in motion; young women showing off their grace and beauty, learning to be alluring. All of them discovering the confidence that performance brings.

The audience was full of parents and grandparents, cousins, uncles, aunts and friends. Tough looking men with calloused hands cradled bouquets of flowers to give to their own dancers. Weary mothers smiled and dreamed great things for their children. Video cameras flickered in the dark. Everyone watching was swept up in the same joy the dancers felt, changed for a while by the alchemy of music mixed with young bodies in an absolute celebration of creation.

An early Saint of the Church, Saint Irenaeus, said 'The glory of God is man fully alive'. If that's true, and I believe it is, then all of the months of practice, culminating in that show, and all of the delight that dance brings to my child and all of the others on that stage, showed forth the glory of God as surely as any Sunday morning worship service.

So I don't care when Elysa is next possessed by spontaneous dance. At the mall, during church, at a funeral or in kindergarten class, it doesn't matter. Because thanks to God, she has the healthy body and inborn desire to do it; and thanks all of her dance teachers, she's learning how.

Magic of Women

There are, in the world, short-sighted people who believe that magic doesn't exist. This is unfortunate. I have seen it, in such times as when a child is rushed to the hospital after he was found gasping and unresponsive at home. His parents, appropriately concerned, are bumfuzzled in the emergency room to see their little one, who was corpse-like an hour before, running down the hall, laughing, dismantling ventilators and singing 'The Star Spangled Banner'.

Magic shows up in nature. It causes snow to fall from crystal blue winter skies, as if transported from another world. Nature's magic causes winds that blow unsuspecting cats off of the porch, leaving them ruffled and annoyed, and brings school closing blizzards the night before unfinished term-papers are due.

But there is another form of magic more commonplace and more powerful. And that is the magic of women. All women have magical powers. These powers cause stoic fathers to practice ballet across the living room floor when compelled by their daughters. This magic later makes young men drop things and mumble incomprehensible words when lovely young things cast their spells. It causes weight-lifting wrestlers to compose sonnets, and turns un-athletic scholars into violent street fighters. This sort of chaos is the result of young magic in young women. It causes a kind of chaos, as unpredictable as the hormonal surges of both sexes in adolescence. It is undisciplined. It can even be as vindictive as it is erotic. My girlfriend once cursed me with an illness for going on vacation without her. I spent my time at Disney World lying in a bed, dizzy from anti-diarrhea medicine.

Later the magic is refined in the wife. A wife has a different kind of magic. It is more controlled. Those who use it well can move a man to purchase a dinette and china instead of plasma TV's, and to attend the wedding of their wife's distant cousin despite having tickets to the Final Four. (That particular potion involves some combination of perfume, high heels and shredded basketballs). New wife magic has its dangers. It can be randomly broadcast and affect unintended targets, resulting in jealousy and infidelity; Cupid's arrows off the mark. But all in all, the magic of young wives is a force for order and stability in the world. The wise among men succumb to it, allowing it to work for them, realizing the old adage, 'happy wife, happy life'.

But this magic is never more wondrous than when it is fully grown in a mother. I have seen this as well. A woman receives enormous doses of it when a child is within her. She is attuned to another realm. She smells things mere humans cannot. She sees germs and dirt where the rest of us would perform surgery without a blink. She looks into the future and sees her child after it is born, and arranges the nursery and the world to accommodate.

After the child is born, a mother has a sway over nature that is indescribable. She can calm a child with colic by whispering magic words (I've listened, but the words had nothing to do with leaving the child for coyotes). She can create a gourmet meal with nothing but a can of pinto beans, some carrots and a package of frozen sausage. And she can find things.

This is my favorite part. As a habitual loser of things, I often turn to my wife for her assistance. Like a psychic in a murder mystery, she has a sense. She once found a well-hidden Taco Bell in a distant city we had never visited, just by wanting Nachos Bell Grande. But her power stems from more than knowing where I usually leave things. I believe in my heart that she retrieves items from the void, and puts them where she wants them. "Did you look for your keys on the kitchen table, dear?"

"Of course I did. I'm not stupid. They weren't there. Nothing was there. It's an empty table."

"Look again". And as I go off to the table, she weaves the spell. "Findicus Keysicus Humiliationes". Poof. The keys are sitting in the middle of the table. I think the cat, her familiar, moved them there. I once threw my keys at that cat, and lost them for six months. Really.

But embarrassment aside, mother magic is ultimately a wondrous and beautiful thing. It is the magic of creating and sustaining life. It is the magic of knowing the hearts of her family, and of touching them for the better. It is the power of peace over chaos; of gentility over anger; and of civilization over the natural barbarity (and everyday confusion) of men and children.

Of all the magic I've witnessed, the magic of women is the most intoxicating, forceful and intense. I have felt its assorted gifts and curses on many occasions, from assorted women. But the maternal variety is magic at it's best. And, as father of four and loser of everything I touch, as one who lives with the most magical of them all, I speak from experience.

Silence is a Commodity

I believe that silence is one of the rarest, most precious things in the world. But nowhere is it more rare than in the world of parenthood. Jan and I crave, but seldom experience, silence until all four of the children are tucked in their beds and lost in blissful, noiseless unconsciousness. We endure it well, I think

I have two children whose noise level is generally manageable. But I have two, my youngest boy and only girl, who were placed on the earth to fill the air with conversation. They aren't necessarily loud without reason. They don't usually scream mindlessly. Elysa howls like a hound when she hears the song, 'Werewolves of London'. Elijah occasionally screams with excitement or rage. But mostly, they talk.

Jan and I are accustomed to non-stop chatter. She is a counselor by training, I'm a physician. Both of us know how to face an endless array of thoughts and ideas, most of which are irrelevant or inappropriate. By way of bizarre example, one of my junior high school classmates approached Jan (whom he had never met) at my Grandfather's funeral and began to discuss the difficulty he and his wife had with their sex lives while trying to get pregnant.

I experience every topic imaginable in the emergency room. I've received criminal confessions from men who believed they were dying, vivid descriptions of lewd acts, disturbing details of physical ailments (from people who weren't actually patients) and mumbled diatribes from people too drunk to know up from down.

But I never understood truly ceaseless conversation until Elijah and Elysa learned to speak. Every sentence that my wife and I direct toward one another is punctuated and footnoted by their interjected ideas and interrogations. Nowhere is this more evident than in the car. When we travel in the car we are hostages. And the price of our ransom is to listen and respond to the varying, winding, distorted and sometimes profound ideas our children put forth.

Those who have children understand this. For those who don't, here's a little transcript from a drive with the kids:

Jan: Honey, how was work last night?

Elijah: Excuse me, excuse me. If the moon fell into the sun, would the sun explode?

Edwin: I don't think so, because it isn't that big. Work was fine, but we were busy with lots of minor injuries.

Jan: I had a good meeting yesterday at school.

Elysa: Excuse me. Papa, excuse me! Um, do you think I'm a princess? Can you hand me my doll? Elijah won't give me that book!

Elijah: She didn't say please. Mama, excuse me Mama, on X-Box, do you know that we reached the highest level? Do you know that my Wizard has 5000 life points? Mama, do you think the Wizard could beat the Emperor on Star Wars?

Jan: Well, I don't know. Probably not, since Emperor Palpatine was a Sith Lord . Elysa, please say please. I think the new curriculum is going to work well. I'm looking forward to teaching...

Elysa: He never says please to me! Mama, Mama, Mama! Excuse me Mama!

Jan: What, WHAT?

Elysa: I...I...I love you!

Jan: I love you too.

Elijah: Do you think that if we could separate all of our atoms that we could walk through walls?

Elysa: Walk through walls, walk through walls, walk through walls!

Elijah: Papa, excuse me, Papa, she's mocking me.

Edwin: Elysa, stop mocking me. I mean, stop mocking your brother. Jan, what do you want for lunch?

Elysa: Oh, Papa, Mama, Papa, can we go to MacDonald's? Or Sushi? Do you love to watch Strawberry Shortcake?

Elijah: Strawberry Shortcake is dumb. Jedi Knights could chop off her head!

Elysa: No! NOOO!

Edwin: Jan, what do you want?

Jan: I want you to turn on the CD player, very, very loud.

We have quiet sometimes. When the kids are away at friends' houses or school. It will be quieter in a few weeks when Elysa starts K-4, and Elijah goes all day to first grade. The mornings will be silent in our house and car. The only sound we'll hear at first will be our hearts beating loudly, terrified by how much we miss the constant noise. Maybe we'll have to start interrupting each other, just to stay in practice.

Teaching Laughter

It was a proud moment in my life when my three boys began walking through the house saying things like, "It's a mere flesh-wound, I've had worse!" Or, "We are the knights who say 'Nee'". I felt my heart swell a little, and a tear formed in the corner of my eye. My sons, at the tender ages of 10, 8 and 6, had become dedicated fans of 'Monty Python and the Search for the Holy Grail.' Knowing her as I do, their sister will be along soon enough, since she has all of the twisted humor that her brothers possess, camouflaged behind blond locks and blue eyes. This delights me, because humor is a gift I want to give them.

Now, every man has some things he wants to teach his children. Every man has some skills that he feels are necessary. The diversity of this world requires different gifts from different fathers, so that subsequent generations are able to keep this old world rolling along to its ultimate conclusion. Some men build things, and their children spend their free hours tinkering with engines, or building birdhouses. Some fathers inculcate a sense of business and economics into their children, so that future captains of industry are learning the ropes early in the game. The list is endless, and I'm glad it is.

I practice medicine. I teach this to my children a little at a time. Things like what to do for bleeding wounds, how to know if someone might be having a heart attack, how to recognize low blood sugar and the location of the spleen (a word my kids find endlessly hilarious). But I can't exactly take them to the hospital and show them. People might feel a little 'creeped out' by tiny 'interns' in white lab coats, poking at their swollen bellies, moving their broken limbs and telling them that they're having a 'Mikodardical Infracalation'. Medicine will have to wait a while.

But I can give them other things. And humor is high on the list. See, when I was younger, I wanted to be either an Air Force navigator, a cartoonist or a stand-up comedian. I kept getting lost in my own house, so navigator was out. My drawings, unlike those of my children, made ancient cave art look like Rembrandt. So comedian kept looking better. However, my parents informed me that that wasn't really a viable option. Either they 1) wanted to make sure I had a solid future with a good income and pension or 2) really didn't think I was funny.

So off I went into medicine. And what did I discover there? Medicine is a giant sit-com. Pre-med students were all nuts who would boil their own limbs in coconut milk and study their cooked flesh if it meant getting another A to add to their GPA. Medical students were freaks who had spent so much time getting into medical school that they forgot to pick up the sense of reality and perspective that they pawned to get there. And residents were repressed, over-educated, hyper-caffeinated lunatics who hadn't had a life in about 8 years. Full-fledged doctors were more of the same, and patients are a treasure trove of laughter in and of themselves.

All of this, along with life as a preacher's kid, has helped to cook up my bizarre sense of humor. And I give it to my children as often as I can. I give them irony and sarcasm, word-plays and slapstick. I give them comic poetry and funny songs. And as often as they're ready, I share with them the movies that have made Jan and me laugh. We have introduced them to the genius of Mel Brooks in 'Young Frankenstein' and 'Spaceballs', the physical humor of 'Harry and the Henderson's' and to the amazing Cohen brothers via 'O Brother Where Art Thou'. The kids have been overheard saying, 'we thought you was a toad'.

I look forward to watching them grow in laughter. There's a lot more I want to share: 'Raising Arizona', 'Blazing Saddles' and tons of other movies and comedians. There is wisdom in humor, and humility in it also. Each of us is, in our own way, a living, breathing comedy. Discovering it takes the pressure off, and helps make this world a little lighter in the midst of the darkness. And there's no time to learn it like childhood, and no guide like a parent who loves to laugh.

Alone with Dora

When my daughter Elysa was about two years old, we took her to her first ever July 4th celebration. The air was sticky warm, and we had all eaten our share of hot dogs and hamburgers, drunk our fill of coke, and had walked to a field where fireworks were streaking into the hazy air above a local church. As we watched, I realized that her grandmother was holding her. Ordinarily, this would not have been much of an issue. Her grandmother loves to hold her. Her grandmother has never dropped her. Elysa, who I expected to hold her little ears in terror as the explosions thumped the air above us, rested in her grandmother's arms comfortably, looked up in the sky with nonchalance, and became quite sleepy.

I, on the other hand, was stunned. I had expected to hold her myself. I had expected she would want me, 'papa, papa', as the rockets red glare and burst in the air. And in my sudden, mid-summer explosion of jealousy, I did not expect to feel irrelevant.

Looking back, I am amazed at the way I can slip from normal to frantic. I can create mountain chains from a single mole's hill. Furthermore, it was all the more ridiculous, considering that I am suddenly faced with the fact that my little girl, my baby girl, slips off to K-4 tomorrow at Oconee Christian Academy, the same school her brothers attend.

The consignment of each of my children to education has been difficult for me. I am selfish by nature, and I can't help the feeling that they are my unique possessions. When I have to send them off into the care of others, I always feel a bit nauseated. I have been weak in the knees every time one of them has, for the first time, donned a new backpack, met a new teacher, discovered new skills and found new friends.

But this time it's a bit harder, for she is my youngest, and the last to enter the hallowed halls of kindergarten. And let's face it.

She and I have the special bond of father and daughter: or as some might call it servant and master.

For four years, she has been mine and her mother's. For four years, we have spent mornings playing or running errands, watching Cinderella movies and counting in Spanish with Dora the Explorer. We have played with dolls and built with blocks. And over those four years, we have seen her change from a newborn ball of pink to a much taller, much more articulate little girl; also in pink. She has transformed slowly but surely into a miniature of her mother, all confidence, grace, beauty and laughter, with a charming but powerful dose of feminine manipulation thrown in for good measure.

In her transformation, I have learned all about her life. I know what colors she will choose, and what music makes her burst into dance. I know the tone of her voice in joy and in fear. And now, others will get to discover these things as well. I grow jealous writing the words.

But, I realize now what I realized shortly after my tiny psychotic episode that summer night. She is mine. And she is not. She is made in the unique image of God, by that same God, who gave her to us for a while. And she is made for other people in addition to her mother and me. She is here to give her grandparents delight. She is here to train her brothers in the ways of women. She is here to find friends and hold their hands in the hallway. It is her destiny to glorify God with her every laugh, her every toss of every strand of her golden hair. She is here, God willing, to love a man one day, and love her children. In short, Elysa is here to bring joy to untold numbers of people in her span on this planet, and we in this house have no right to hoard her wonder.

I realize, as I consider it, that this is not a sudden event. We have introduced her to the world bit by bit, and she is ready for more. From family and friends to church and dance class, she moves with easy grace. Tomorrow, I will kiss her on the cheek as she bounces off to greater things and moves her beauty to the larger world.

But I won't like it. And I may just have to watch Dora by myself.

Christmas Can't Be Rushed

When I was a child I would lie underneath the covers on Christmas night with a small transistor radio and ear-piece and listen to Christmas carols on local radio stations until midnight. That was when most stations returned to normal format. This always, without fail, broke my childhood heart. Because the holiday was simply too fleeting for me. I wanted to take it all in; to absorb as much of the season as I possibly could. "We now return to our regular format" was a painful concession to the ordinary and an abdication of things bright and glorious.

I still face the same problem. After Thanksgiving I am delighted as stations play holiday music and decorations appear on homes and in public places. I look for the chill in the air, I watch for winter clouds and revert to my childhood in West Virginia when I try to detect the smell of snow in the air (a largely useless skill in South Carolina, to be sure).

The shopping, the parties, the lights, the cold, all give me special joy. So much more with small children who are learning the story of Christ's birth, who are expecting Santa and are glowing with the same love of the season as their mother and father.

But along with the wonder, Christmas still holds that youthful frustration for me, in the form of my continued attempt to encompass the significance of the season. I suspect that even in my childhood I was reaching for some primal understanding. Unfortunately, the ability to see the meaning and the ability to grasp it are two separate things.

However, my pursuit of Christmas has brought me an important insight. Meaning is a precious thing. It comes at a price to everyone and the price is usually time and effort. But introspection and meditation have become too time consuming, too uncertain, because our civilization is addicted to speed and ease. We eat fast food, drive through the pharmacy and tap our fingers in annoyance when the modem takes more than a few seconds to connect us around the world. Our spirituality is answered by platitudes in self-help CD's and our parenting is compressed into the travesty of "quality time."

The uneasy reality is that essential things cannot be rushed or made simple. And meaning, whether it is the meaning of Christmas or the meaning of our lives, is a thing that will not come without effort and inner struggle. In fact it may require a lifetime and may only come to us when we have surrendered the quest in hopeless exhaustion.

Nevertheless this can be a time of hope for those who feel frustrated and harried by their search for depth in the mad press of Christmas. After Christmas, the Church calendar comes to the time of Epiphany, which celebrates the visit of the Magi, wise men of the East. Not actually kings, the Magi may have been astrologers from Persia or Arabia who followed the star to Bethlehem. We see them in nativity scenes, but scholars believe, and the Bible suggests, that they arrived later to worship the Christ child.

"The Story of the Other Wise Man," by Henry van Dyke is the tale of Artaban, the Magi who was delayed by good deeds for some thirty years in his search for the infant King. When at last he finds him it is at His crucifixion. Our modern search may not end so dramatically but it should be no surprise that the pilgrimage for things of value may lead us to the manger by routes we did not expect to travel, over spans of time far longer than those we imagined and infinitely longer than those allotted by our calendars or shopping days.

Oktoberfest

When the shadows have lengthened and autumn has settled firmly on the foothills of the Blue Ridge Mountains, the time of magic is near. When the night air is cool, the sweaters begin to appear from boxes in closets and children's cheeks are pink with the wind, the magic is closer. But the third weekend in October, in Walhalla, South Carolina, the magic arrives.

It's difficult to describe. All year long, for those of us who live nearby and drive past Sertoma Field on Highway 183, it is like athletic fields in any community, where t-ball, baseball, soccer and football are played. It's a place with playgrounds, swings and a walking trail. There are benches and tables for picnics and a carpet of lush, green grass. My family and I have had many good times there.

But on the third weekend of October every year, something happens. I've long suspected it is tied to constellations, the moon, the tides and the cool breath of impending winter. But on that Friday night Oktoberfest begins. Just before the sun goes down we load the children into the car, drive to the field and push strollers up the slight rise from where we park. As we crest the hill, Sertoma becomes something entirely different. It becomes a place of carnival rides, arts and crafts booths, German music, sausage and beer.

Even more it becomes a place of light. There is light everywhere. It shoots up into the fall sky like a beacon to the universe speaking of joy and wonder. The light fills the place, illuminating the hillsides and creating so many shadows among the tents and trailers along the periphery that the place is transformed and nearly unrecognizable.

The road leading to the field is always packed with cars; the head-lights that seem to go on for miles lend the whole event a sense of urgency, a sense that all over the area people love

Oktoberfest for the childlike delight it provides, and that more than wanting it, they need it. Maybe they need it for the same reasons I do, because it ushers in autumn for our county and because the skies are clear and the stars bright. Maybe they need it because it is the essence of community where grudges and differences seem to be suspended for three days. Or because the children become sweetly insane elves allowed to stay up far later than normal, forced to eat cotton candy, funnel cake, candy-apples and other delights and driven to spin on rides until their laughing heads wobble with centrifugal force. Maybe everyone, adults and children alike, love it because when they crest that hill as we do they are transported into a place of pure wonder. And because they know that when they drive past the same place the next week it will be gone. It's bittersweet, like so many of life's deepest pleasures.

This is a source of annual joy to my family. In fact, we have enjoyed Oktoberfest since the first time we visited the area many years past. It was one of our reasons for moving to Walhalla. I suspect that we felt the transformation even then as the common became uncommon for a while and the normal geography of a place that we didn't even know became warm and welcome.

Oktoberfest is a place of dreams. Last year, while my children slipped and cackled down a large slide already begging to go again, I had a waking dream. The memory is hazy and my notes about it are heaven knows where, but I believe I dreamed that they were all grown and healthy and that I had brought them and their children to enjoy the same magic that seemed not yearly but eternal. Or maybe I dreamed that their childhood was the eternal thing and that as long as we played in the shelter of that little valley, surrounded by sounds, smells and tastes of delight, bathed in flashing neon and the cool of October, they would never grow up and Jan and I never grow old.

Like all dreams it was part place, part fear, part hope. But God willing, every year I'll return to the semi-reality of the magical little field on Highway 183 to refresh my sense of wonder and recharge my dreams. I'll hold my wife's hand, spoil the children (and eventually the grandchildren), and enjoy the mystery once again, surrounded by the ones I love the most.

Blind Man's Child

I met a man who identified himself only by his disability. Young and blind, he has a child he has never seen with his own eyes. He lives in a world driven and defined by light, shape and color; a world of height, width, depth and time. He lives in a world of the four dimensions, but cannot see any of those visible lines which make earth the world of sight, and which can so easily imprison the blind; or at least their hearts. And so, trapped as he is in certain iron-clad limitations, he came to see himself only in terms of tragedy.

He told me, with deep sadness, that he was of no use to his child. He believed that he could never play with her properly, could never be the father that she needed; a father with working eyes who could watch her in the sunlight, who could play with her freely and wildly as fathers want to do. He could see only one thing, and it wasn't light or his child; he could see only what he did not have; only what he could never be.

But it is the common fate of us all. We seldom see ourselves for what we are. We are far too busy seeing ourselves for what we are not. In the realm of the material, we are convinced that we are not wealthy enough, or that we are not bright enough. We believe our actions and works are worthless, and that we would be useful only if we had the talents and gifts of others all around us, who seem so bright and shiny. Even in the world of the spirit, we see ourselves only as sinners, only as the inadequate; seldom as the unique children of a God who loves us whoever we may be, whatever our strengths our failures.

So it's no surprise that, born into a world where humans see only their limitations, my young, blind friend fights a constant battle with despair. He feels stricken, weakened, and pointless. But there is good news. He has a chance to be something great for his child. That young man, whose eyes are no longer tunnels of light, can live in all four dimensions just as surely as the rest of us do. And what he sees as weakness can become an unimaginable gift.

Because, when his daughter is in his arms, he will know her by touch. He will know every contour, every joint, every bone, every rash, and each scar by the feel of his loving hand. The transformation of her skin from baby to adult will pass beneath his sensing fingers and his mind will catalog all of it.

He will know the way she shakes with laughter and the way she heaves with sobs. He will feel her grow, and will, without any need for sight, be the comfortable place she comes when she is tired or happy, sad or thrilled.

When his daughter enters the room, he will know the sound of her footfall as surely as he would know the color of her eyes. Her breath will be as clear to him as the light on her hair would be, and the tones of her voice will betray as much as her facial expressions could ever reveal.

He will delight in the smell of her freshly shampooed hair and washed skin. He will know the smell of her breath when she is ill and the smell of her summer skin when she is glistening with childhood sweat. And the taste of her cheeks will be sweet to him when he kisses her good morning and good night. The taste of her tears will fill him with love and mercy.

My friend, if he desires, can know his child in ways the sighted seldom explore. More to the point, his love need not be restricted by the senses, or their absence. If he chooses, then his children will remember him, not for his closed eyes but for his open heart. And they will know him as a man courageous enough to walk around his perceptions of what he was not, in order to embrace all that he is.

Diabetes made my young friend blind. Please support the Juvenile Diabetes Research Foundation's annual Walk for the Cure. For information about the walk, or to donate, go to www.jdrf.org.

Home Defense

While walking around my house one night, I realized just how dangerous the average home is. I'm not talking about power tools, firearms, poisons and all that. No, I'm thinking of threats far more insidious, far more camouflaged and often more painful. I'm thinking of two major groups of dangers; toys and pets. Now some doctors would make this the focus of a safety education program, and would endlessly lecture their patients on safety this, safety that, blah, blah, blah.

I look at it another way. My house is virtually intruder proof. I thought about it one day. And as I thought about it, I imagined a bad guy trying to get into my home in the dark.

First, he comes to the driveway, where the dogs bark ferociously and subject him to one of three treatments. If they perceive him to be a threat (as they perceived my father-in-law the Halloween he approached the children in a mask, carrying a scythe), he may be bitten.

If they smell food, grease or condiments, they will mob him, covering him in dog drool. This may seem benign, but if later he receives a skin wound of any sort, a nasty dog-mouth infection may result! Biological warfare for the home, as it were.

On some nights, however, the dogs engage in a more stealthy defense of our hearth and home. Highly trained for security, our six mutts of assorted size will strategically place themselves around the yard, on the steps and in front of the door and pretend to be asleep. Oh, it's effective. Because rather than biting, this highly effective 'passive defense' arrangement causes the intruder to trip and fall onto rocks or porch, effectively dislocating or fracturing assorted body parts. Years of training have made this their preferred method of attack. Years of training and over-eating, that is.

Fine, let's suppose that our committed intruder manages to circumvent our canine special forces with some cruel technique like, well, petting them. He still has to face the cats. Inside, the cats roam the house at night like scary little…cats. But their ruse is also complex. At night, when they are most frisky, they have been known to attack ankles from below, and attack the tops of human heads from above on the stairs. This is enough to make the unsuspecting have dangerous heart arrhythmias in the night.

Next, there's the old 'step on my tail' trick, in which the cat allows his tail to be crunched by a human foot, and then proceeds to scream like a 'cat out of hell'. I have experienced this before, and I am certain that it took years off of my life, and several lives off of the cat. This alone might make our intruder leave (and see his cardiologist), since it is loud enough to alert the entire house and all the dogs.

Last, the cats have another technique. Cats are 'history's furry little assassins'. Many men and women have met their demise as cats intertwined themselves between their legs under the pretense of wanting food, when in fact it was an act as aggressive and cold-blooded as any crocodile attack. The malefactor trips and stumbles, hitting his head on a counter or falling on a sharp object. The cat licks himself quietly, satisfied with a night's work, and displays that 'I have no idea what happened' look on his face.

Of course, some felons understand the power of a can of tuna. The cats might be overcome. There are still toys. I believe that Legos may be the most deadly item in any home. If our criminal decides to be quiet and go barefoot, they will send him into spasms of intense pain. With shoes, they'll roll on the carpet, twisting legs and causing gravity to have its way. Legos on hardwood floors result in sudden ice-skating, with results of orthopedic proportion.

But we have other assorted items on the floor and steps. Our man will face toy tanks with wheels, toy knights with upturned, razor sharp plastic weapons, rearranged furniture, and booby-traps made of battery powered imitation firearms that sound like the real thing. He will have to navigate Matchbox cars and praying dolls, comic books and video game cartridges. It will be a night not soon forgotten.

So who needs a security system! Get yourself some highly trained dogs and cats, and hire some children to scatter assorted plastic and wooden implements around the house. Only the bravest, and most balanced, will survive the attempt on your home.

Family Kingdom

A family is a small kingdom. Their house is the castle, to be cliché. It is mutable, its location flexible. But the royalty, the humans that live within it, define the kingdom. Small children understand this very well. The idea of father as king, mother as queen, themselves as princes and princesses, resonates inside their hearts. It becomes, in the best situations, a kind of fairy tale made real.

The family kingdom is a complex dynamic. Too often considered authoritarian, with a king who does just what he wants and others who bend to his will, it is really, in its glory, a place where the king leads and protects his royal family, always looking for ways to increase its honor. It is a place where the good queen civilizes and counsels her king and her children, and is herself treated with gentility and respect. And it is a place where children get wisdom, nobility and learning without fear.

This kingdom is meant to be a safe haven. The basic family unit, in more modern terms, is designed as a small enclave where couples come together in love, and in that love support one another. The family is a thing through which the whole world is made safer by small increments. Ideally, it leaves the world richer by populating it with sane, productive, creative citizens. Ultimately, each generation supplies society with young men and women who go on to create new kingdoms of their own.

But not all kingdoms are good, not all are safe, and even the best kingdom is always in danger of collapse, either from inside or out. Anyone who has read history can cite examples of the fall of kingdoms, good and bad. There were kingdoms that decayed because subjects were treated worse than enemies and ignorance was desirable to promote slavery. There were kingdoms of awful intrigue, where emperors were murdered by princes for power and empresses beheaded for producing no heirs. There were kingdoms so horrible that the only option was escape. There were also royal families in which monarchs were not really cruel, just heartless or without joy. And there were golden kingdoms destroyed by jealous invaders.

Not all families are safe kingdoms either. In medicine, we see their citizens every day. We see lonely, overworked wives whose husbands left them for the excitement of what they saw as a kind of dark rebirth, disguised in the language of passion and adventure. We see devoted husbands whose wives were tired of marriage and moved on to different lovers, led away by the phantom of false romance. And we meet children whose kingdoms collapsed around them, through no fault of their own, but who always wonder what they did to make their dream end.

What all children want, what all adults want, are the defining boundaries of love. Everyone desires the interlocking arms of parents and children whose love for one another is so great it flows over onto everyone who touches them. What everyone wants is a kingdom intact.

Nonetheless, like dangerous empires, some marriages have to end. Violence and substance abuse drive husbands, wives and children to safer lands. Deep betrayal and distrust also end families. In these settings, children and wounded parents have to find security and peace of mind.

But in too many cases marriages end, beautiful kingdoms dissolve, for reasons that are poorly examined and for imaginary dreams that never become as real as the life left behind. In the end, when the ink is on the page, the agreements arrived at, the houses sold, the money divided, the children parceled out, what really happens is much more painful.

Coping with My Fear of the Night

I work full time nights. There is a method to my madness. By doing this, I have more total days off each month to spend with my wife and children. Nights in the emergency department are seldom as slow as I'd like. They usually challenge either my skill or my patience. But even more, they challenge my faith. Because it seems that over the years I have developed a growing sense of vague anxiety. It isn't debilitating. And maybe it is just fatherhood. But every night when I leave for work, I fear. And, as I fear I allow doubt to creep into my thoughts and erode my faith like a slow growing cancer.

I suppose the practice of emergency medicine in modern times is enough to engender anxiety. Although I do not work at an urban trauma center, I trained at one. Furthermore, I see enough terrible, frightening things to cause anyone to fear. What I do not see, I imagine. Even a partial list would be exhaustive, but among the things that I fear most are violence or accidents involving my family, and medical errors or failures on my part that might cost someone their life. However, over the past year I have discovered a strategy. It came from two sources of inspiration.

First, one day as I was thinking about how many of my patients are frustrating or difficult, I seemed to hear God speak to me. He said, ever so quietly, "You take care of my children, and I'll take care of yours". I think he meant that while all of the patients I see are his sons and daughters, some of them, perhaps the most frustrating ones, are his problem children. They are his prodigals. And for some, my partners and I are the only persons who give them medical care. Some of them are trapped by substance abuse, some by domestic violence. Others are mired in poverty or ignorance. But whatever the problem he still loves them. And when they are sick or injured, he wants them cared for not just with competence, but with compassion. He seemed to be explaining an arrangement, as it were. Just as I want God to give mercy to my wife and children (and myself), he wants me to give mercy to these, his special children. In the midst of caring for them, this reality gives me pause, and helps me to realize that their father is the king.

Second, I began to see that prayer is the antidote to fear and nourishment for faith. But, the hectic pace of raising three young sons and a daughter combined, with a full time practice, often makes prolonged periods of prayer and reflection very difficult. However, I came to realize, by reading Richard Foster's book "Prayer", that these things are possible if we accept that they may look a little different, or happen in unique ways that fit our lifestyles. Sometimes they can only come twice a week, sometimes several times, but in shorter bursts.

With this in mind, I developed the habit of praying in my car before leaving for work each night. Sitting in the dark, I pray with two basic intentions. First, I pray for the safety and peace of my family throughout the night. Not that God doesn't also protect them when I'm there, he does, but the night carries a sense of uncertainty that is not present when the sun is up. I think that the Psalmist understood this well, when he said, in Psalm 91: 5-6 "You will not fear the terror of night...nor the pestilence that stalks in the darkness...." I ask for him to watch over each of them as I list them by name. Next, I pray for the patients that I will see in the coming hours. I ask that God keep them from critical illness or injury. But, whatever their problem, I ask him to guide me and make me capable and kind as I try to meet their needs.

Now when I leave for work, I have this time of comfort. It gives me peace. It eases my anxiety on virtually every level, personal and professional. I know I do not deserve any special protection from Him. But I ask for it anyway. And because he is my father, I trust him. As a father, I know that just the chance to talk puts my sons' and daughters' fears away. I suppose it should be no surprise that the same is true for me.

So, I'm coming to grips with my anxiety. It was important first to embrace and accept it. As physicians, we have been too often educated in an environment that denied our own fear, branding it weakness. But even Christ himself must have known fear, though he was not possessed by it. So, if fear troubles you, turn to the author of peace. And learn to practice, and live, in the presence of your fears without staring too long at them. They are, after all, mostly shadows of much smaller things. And our Lord can handle them all.

Date Night Romance

Jan and I had a date last week. We try to do it weekly when we can. We bring in a sitter and leave the children behind for a few hours so that we can have a quiet dinner and maybe a movie. This date night was especially romantic, beginning in a local restaurant and ending...with grocery shopping.

Date or no date, you have to have groceries. But walking around the store, laughing and joking with my wife of 15 years, I was reminded that married life is a hybrid. Real love is romance mixed with laundry; passionate kisses overtop of angry toddlers trying to pry the lovers apart, screaming, 'no kissing, no kissing!'

So I thought, how would our date night look, written as a romance? Let's see...

Edwin's hand brushed against Jan's as he reached for the shopping cart. She smiled, and tossed her purse inside. As they walked into the store, her mind raced with a million thoughts. 'Does he feel the same desire as I do? Does he find me attractive? Does he want...a huge bag of M and M's?' With a coy turn of her head, she looked at him. 'We need cereal'.

Edwin felt his heart race. Cereal. The words he had longed for her to say. There's only so much Special K a man can endure, week after week. He wondered what sort of cereal this fiery woman would pick. Would she be practical? Would it be Cheerios? Would it be, heaven forbid, some kind of granola freshly scraped from a grain silo? NO! She traced her slender finger along the boxes as his breath quickened. Her red nail polish was bright against the assorted colors of cartoon characters. She lingered over Rice Krispies, she paused at Muselix. Then she grasped the box of Lucky Charms with passionate intensity and tossed it into the buggy. Edwin felt himself sweat. Lucky Charms! Joy of joys. This was a real woman.

He reached for her, needing to pull her close, when he heard the scraping sound of a large cart. 'Excuse me please', said the young man stocking the shelves. Jan slipped from his reach and disappeared around the corner.

'I love the way you pick breakfast food', he whispered when he caught up to her. 'I know', she replied, and she leaned forward, breathing in his ear. 'We need milk; can you get some?' Edwin kissed her hand and left for the dairy aisle, trying to locate the 1% milk while Jan made her way toward boxed pizza. He returned to her with three gallons of milk, which made the relatively small muscles of his forearms bulge under their combined weight. 'Nice forearms', Jan said.

'Thanks. I work out at least once a month.'

She flirted back. 'You can tell. You can definitely tell'.

They walked further and loaded the cart with the various items they needed and also the things they desired. Thinking about the rest of the evening, Edwin suddenly remembered the powerful effect that Diet Coke had on Jan. The way it kept her from dozing off in the mid-afternoon from sheer exhaustion. He loaded a 12 pack onto their cart. 'How much?' She asked him, looking over her sunburned shoulder. Edwin could see that this woman was both beautiful and practical. '$3.88'. 'Just get one'. He obeyed and slipped next to her, putting his arm around her waist.

'I love this. I love our time together. This place, your dress, the smell of freshly opened boxes of produce, it's intoxicating!' He wondered if she felt the same, or if she was simply humoring him as she flipped through the coupons in her hand, her silver bracelet glinting in the soft glow of fluorescent lighting, its hum like background music for their interlude.

Looking up at him, her eyes became deep with emotion and she casually pushed the buggy away, nearly wiping out an elderly shopper with a walker. 'Sorry!' she cried as she retrieved the nearly 150 pounds of groceries.

'Where were we?'

'Right here,' he said as he kissed her, fiercely and briefly, before tripping into a display of canned vegetables.

She helped him up, barely able to control her laughter. 'I can't take this anymore! Edwin, you have to take me...you have to take me right now...to the stationary. The kids are starting school, and we need, well, school stuff.'

She was beautiful when she said 'school stuff' and when she mentioned the children. She was elegant when she called the babysitter to make sure that she wasn't tied in a corner.

Jan was everything Edwin could want. And as she swayed off to the other side of the store Edwin realized that he was the luckiest man alive. Because there was the woman he loved, there was the cereal he wanted and dead ahead was the magazine rack, where she had been temporarily distracted. There was food in the cart, a beautiful woman by his side, children sleeping at home and now, chick magazines with relationship quizzes to take.

What a night it had been. What a night it would be.

Ancestor's Prayer

This time of year our children spend lots of time revisiting the trials of those brave folks who landed in Plymouth. My kids have all gone over the story too many times to recount. Whether or not any of our family's ancestors can be traced to that event is not clear. But it doesn't matter. That episode in our national history is a kind of metaphor for all of us; Thanksgiving is a remembrance of a profound cultural event that stands independent of blood-lines.

But as we go over the tale again, and as we sit down to eat too much with our families, I wonder how often we forget just how far back our families go, and just what they would think if they saw us now. Family memories in modern times are as short as our collective attention spans.

Of course, we store some pictures, either the way my family did (in large boxes, with vague scribbles on the back of each one), or as some more aggressive, more obsessive folks do, in committed albums with pre-printed captions and all the trimmings. But our pictures or video-tapes don't usually go back much more than two or three generations.

We probably do worse with stories than with images. Someone in each of our families typically knows a few of the trials of our more illustrious ancestors. We may learn from these archivists who survived this battle, or who perished in that epidemic. We might know someone who knew someone who knew a president. But the tales never go further back than one or two centuries, and are always sporadic bits of information, and even then are usually only the most fascinating events and connections in our family lines. And the vast majority of the names and faces from whom we are descended are lost like dandelion seeds on the winds of time.

When I look at my life, and at my wife and children, and when I consider the great expanse of time, I am always amazed. However we view this life, whether as the product of eons of evolution or as the result of God's direct hand on Adam 5000 years ago, each of us can trace his family back beyond the bounds of imagination. Each of us is the product of mighty efforts of survival against tremendous odds, desperate travels for food and brutal battles to escape cruelty. Each of us sits around our Thanksgiving table with historical myopia. We so wish we could connect ourselves to the Mayflower, when our family stories, for thousands of years, are made up of men and women whose struggles made that little trip to Massachusetts look like a Carnival Cruise.

All of us are descended from heroes and scoundrels, from slaves and kings, prostitutes and prophets. Our DNA bears the marks of more people than we can possibly dream, whose lives were both wonderful and terrible. And I suspect that our dreams bear some of what they left us as well.

I often imagine them when I read a story from the past, or when my wife tells me something from antiquity as she prepares to teach a Latin class. I think of them when I watch history documentaries. I think of them as I put my children safe in their beds. And often, on cold nights beneath crystalline starry nights, I look up and imagine them doing the same, hoping and praying beneath stars that have changed only imperceptibly between then and now.

When I see them in my minds eye, they are resting from their labors or struggles. They are Romans under warm Italian skies, or Britons suffering under Rome. They are children of Mongols, or children of the Twelve Tribes. They are women who have born children and men plowing the ground with sticks and stones. They are wounded, ill, heartbroken, enslaved or indentured. But some of them are successful, ruling over others from Athens, from the snowy plains of Russia or the forests of Germany. They live in ancient India, the Congo or along the Nile. The may be servants of Persian kings or travelers on Arctic seas.

But they look at the stars and ask their gods to bless their children, and children's children, and give them something better, someday. A freedom, a hope, a blessing they do not have. And as I sit down to pray this Thursday, I need to give thanks to God for answering their prayers before he ever heard mine.

Apocalypse of Plastic and Paper

Ever since my childhood, I have thought about the end of time. Like many churches in the seventies and eighties, my home church went through a time of ardent prophecy study. We endured predictions that the rapture would certainly come within a decade. We watched Christian movies depicting persecution and apocalypse, and I was fairly convinced, through small tracts left for searching young minds, that the end wound come in my time, it would involve communists and nuclear war, and it would really impede my enjoyment of my teenage years.

I am a grown man of almost 41 years now. The teenage years were not all that exciting, and I'm quite enjoying my wife and family. The world looks different now, though not any less perilous than when I was younger. Terrorists have replaced communists as the prevalent threat, and I worry that my enjoyment of retirement may be disrupted by biological warfare and daily harassment by radical Islamic elements, who conspire to steal my walker and prescription drug card.

In general, though, I'm less concerned with the end of things than before. Because I've realized that the world will probably end in a way never imagined by anyone else, and I'm resigned to my role as prophet of doom. After years of intense speculation and constant observation, after hearing four decades of prophetic errors hurled from pulpits and books, I now believe that encoded in the book of Revelations are the words 'and there was another horseman, and behind him there trailed endless bits of paper and plastic, and the world was covered up completely by them.'

Father of four and recipient of far too much mail, I am pretty certain the world will end when we are up to our eyeballs in plastic objects and junk-mail. As far as the plastic objects, I believe that two main groups are in league with the dark prince;

toy manufacturers and the fast food industry. For paper, I blame professional organizations and mass marketing companies.

Toys are shrinking all the time. My daughter Elysa has Barbie dolls that are visible and manageable. But Barbie's accoutrements, her brushes, her mirrors, her infernal shoes and jewelry are all sizes, from small to microscopic. And now Elysa has a fascination with even smaller dolls, and they have even smaller shoes and purses. Check any corner of the house, any part of the car; there they are, taking over everything.

But to blame Elysa would be unfair. The boys have plastic knights and soldiers, plastic animals, plastic Star Wars figures, Disney characters, GI Joe parts, Matchbox cars and every other imaginable small thing, along with the small weapons and gear that go with already small things. And, clear minion of evil, Legos by the thousands. Those sadistic manufacturers of Legos ..force me to walk a gauntlet of pointed objects every night when I check on my children in their bedroom. Tiny landmines, they cause unbelievable pain and unfortunate words when they penetrate the sole of my bare foot at midnight. This is simply tangible evidence of their evil.

In cahoots with the toy manufacturers are the fast-food industry folks, who insert movie and television linked products into their assorted kids' meals. Children, lured by this dark magic, will ignore expensive toys and go out of their little minds for a two-inch tall figure of Mr. Incredible. These items also populate our house and car. And between all of them, I feel the air being squeezed from my lungs as they rise higher and higher, progressively taking over everything.

Not to be ignored, the marketing industry leaves me with more than unwanted e-mail. Traditionalists remain who send me metric tons of mail for everything from exercise equipment (to remind me that I'm out of shape) to offers for loans I don't need and letters from lobbies I do not care to support. But those things are all subterfuge. The real goal is to fill my house with paper I can't get rid of and contribute to the deadly crush of small objects and paper that will signal the end of the world as we know it.

Future civilizations may excavate our remains and find us like the citizens of Pompeii, finally overwhelmed by a sea of mail and plastic, hands reaching up for air, lungs filled with tiny light sabers and Barbie make-up cases. I see some curled on the ground next to confused dogs, clutching ads for Enzyte. I see our children, forever resting in molds formed by Dora the Explorer Legos. Archeologists will refer to it as the 'small object apocalypse', and museums will be dedicated to preservation of our tragic artifacts.

Robert Frost said, 'Some say the world will end in fire, some say ice'. Clearly he didn't live long enough to see how it would really go down. Come to think of it, fire or ice sound less humiliating.

Christmas Safari

Last week Jan and I went on our yearly Christmas shopping trip. Each year, we leave the children with their good Aunt Julie and we head off to points distant to make our annual gift acquisitions.

I have long been a fan of safari stories, and on some level, Christmas shopping is much the same. You go far from home, you wander through a kind of jungle filled with economic predators, you bag the items you can handle/afford, and you try to get away before something kills your bank account.

Our first stop on the Christmas Safari was in the expensive land of electronics. There, we stalked the aisles for the tiny, but financially unpredictable 'MP-3 Player'. It was an amazing place. The sounds of the electronic jungle beeped, whirred and whistled all around. Mighty bands of plasma televisions grazed on one wall and flocks of music CD's rested quietly in metal nests. Warily, digital camcorders recorded our every step like patient vultures.

When we located our prey, it was sitting quietly on a shelf with the rest of the MP-3 players, its trophy price-tag waving proudly in the air like antlers. Our guide, a kind and patient man who had led many such safaris over the Christmas season, explained what we would need to do to handle such a complicated beast. 'It sure looks small,' we whispered from our hiding place, 'where does all the music go?' Patiently, our guide laughed (believing we were joking). Then, with the technical insight of Jethro and Ellie-May Clampett we asked again, 'No, seriously, where does the music go?' He smiled and explained all of the wonders of this not so rare, but much sought-after beast. It was a good hunt, but I'm not going to say whether we dressed and skinned it or not, since my child may read this account.

Another of our forays into the wilderness of Christmas shopping landed us in the vast republic of 'Haywoodmall'. There, the hunting was good, but it was difficult not to be bowled over by the thousands of other persons stalking gifts. Like the opening day of deer season, there were thousands of people; and a very real danger of being accidentally carried off as a present. The sights and smells of such a wondrous land can be overwhelming and amazing, as well. We ate pretzels and soup, prepared by the local natives who are always eager to lift the cash of those hunting gifts.

The gifts available there are many and wondrous, as well as bizarre, and we wandered about for some time, credit cards and cash safely holstered, marveling at those purchases made by others. For instance, who buys the little toy dogs that appear locked in eternal sleep, but are actually moulds covered in bunny fur? They look as if someone took a puppy, snuffed it out, and dipped it in liquid nitrogen. And how many men need combination sock racks/tire gauges/poker-chip holders? Christmas brings out odd species to hunt, and no doubt results in even more odd looks when packages are opened on Christmas morning.

Jan and I also explored the vast forests and plains of many book stores. These are places where we have had many successful stalks, but where (as always) strange voodoo magic threatened to hold us for hours longer than we intended. We could feel the spell descend upon us. 'Honey, we...have...to...go', 'I know, but this section of children's books...I can't escape. And the historical novels!' Ultimately, it was hunger that broke the spell and left us only partially impoverished in the process of buying books. But before we could settle into our camp for lunch, we visited the game preserve called 'Burlingtoncoat', where untold numbers of confused persons roamed about stalking and buying heavy winter coats for people who live in South Carolina, where winter is less a season than a theory.

I suppose the culmination of our journey was in the kingdom of 'Toyzrus'. There, the hunting was more like shooting passenger pigeons in the days when the sky was dark with the things. Toys were everywhere, and they called out. 'take me, buy me, your children need me!' We are now, however, seasoned hunters of Christmas gifts. We didn't buy nearly as many things impulsively as we would have a few years ago.

While there, we did watch as parents new to the Christmas Safari season loaded their baskets with everything imaginable, because when new children are born to new parents, the result is like, well, it's like goat season at the petting zoo. They buy everything. We smiled quietly to ourselves as well-meaning parents snuck up on brightly colored blocks and dolls meant to stimulate their children's minds, and as even older parents purchased 'educational toys'. In our experience, the 'educational' species always end up ignored in the corner as our own children hit each other with the boxes.

While we were in 'Toyzrus', shopping for the eleven children on our extended list, we received a call from our four-year-old daughter. Apparently now a headhunter, she said 'Mama, I want one of those decapitated Barbie heads you put make-up on, OK?' How do you argue with that? She asks for a decapitated head, so she can learn a trade and be ready for beauty school? We found a decapitated head immediately. You can't go wrong with the word decapitated.

Before our hunt was over, we found something else. Despite worries about the end of Christmas as we know it, despite the bizarre mix of capitalism and faith that Christmas has become, its spirit is alive and well. We saw it in our fellow gift hunters, and in the delightful conversations that our 'shopping guides', aka salespersons, and 'food preparing natives', aka waitresses, shared with us about their own families. Christmas, dear friends, is alive and well on every level whether or not the world is offended by it.

We returned home exhausted and exhilarated. It was another successful journey into the wilds of shopping. We were almost completely out of ammo/money. The children were unconscious. Aunt Julie was not bound or gagged, and was still in possession of her sanity. Our tags were filled, and we dragged home some good cheer and joy to boot. A Christmas safari doesn't get any better than that.

I Want To Be Santa Claus

I want to be Santa Claus. It seems an appealing career. I'm not terribly overweight, but I do love cookies. I could fill out that red suit in no time fat...I mean no time flat. I like snow and have always wanted to visit the North Pole. I enjoy Christmas music and with the right icy castle, the right reindeer, the right staff of busy elves and my wife by my side as Mrs. Claus, I think I could give it a go. I don't think she would be very excited about being plump and white haired, so we could probably make an exception. (Besides, I've seen some 'Mrs. Claus' costumes in catalogs that I'd much prefer to see her wear). The children, all avid toy lovers, would most certainly want to be in the business. Forget medicine! Fetch me my sleigh!

The main reason I'd like to be Santa is that I like to give gifts. My wife says that for this reason alone, I would make a good Kris Kringle. I love is knowing what a few people desire, knowing what moves them or makes them smile, then providing that thing. If I had Santa's budget, Santa's magic, Santa's apparent time travel capabilities and Santa's obvious omniscience, I could really have a good time.

I'm always sad when I know that people receive gifts from the ones who should known them best, but the gifts have no meaning. Gifts are sometimes limited by finances, of course, but that's not what I mean. I'm talking about times when gifts that should be meaningful are meaningless because the giver didn't take the time to know the heart of the recipient.

I hate knowing that children are ignored by parents who are too busy, or too drunk, too self-occupied or too stoned to care. I hate knowing that mothers get sweeper attachments and fathers receive socks, when what they wanted were violin lessons and a Golden Retriever puppy for duck hunting.

But when it comes to giving gifts, it seems that the best things are seldom things at all. If I were Santa, I would want the power to give those gifts that resonate in the halls of the heart. Because people are desperate for their hearts' desires to be known and filled. We are seldom honest with our loved ones about what we truly want. Maybe because we are seldom honest with ourselves. And maybe, because we have spent our lives so occupied with busy-ness and entertainment that we've never bothered to look inside our own selves.

Having spent some time around people, a lot of people, I think I know what I would be dispensing if I were Santa. I would muster all of my magic and give things elemental. I would give freedom to people enslaved by drugs, by food and by the cruel words of others that hold them down. I would give them liberation from the terror of self, by showing them that all of the bad things they think inside their own minds about themselves are false. I would let them wake up, check their stockings by the fire, and suddenly see themselves beautiful and capable, strong and good. I would lift depression like a cloud blown on a winter wind.

I would give children the attention and genuine affection of their parents. I would give relief and hope to those suffering with the pain of diseases, so that on Christmas morning they felt not an ounce of discomfort. I would give back the missing children, and restore the relationships of estranged families. I would renew the passion of marriages that have been mere rote, elevate them from misery to delight and let Christmas morning be like a reunion of lost lovers.

If I were Santa, I would visit the dying with visions of heaven so wonderful that their fear was banished like darkness before the rising dawn of Christmas morning. I would let men and women wake to see their dreams as possibilities, and give them some thing, some opportunity, some chance meeting that would send them laughing into the rest of their lives, doing what God made them to do with absolute abandon. If I were Santa, I would even comfort the arthritic bones of old dogs, so they could chase one another once more.

If I were Santa, I would do so much. But I'm not. I guess the best gifts are still up to each of us for now. Trust me, when I get the job, you'll know.

Words and MP3 players

Technology (in league with Santa Claus) has done me a favor in the form of the MP-3 player. Sam, our oldest, has received one for Christmas. Though some people consider their i-pod as critical as a pacemaker, these things are new to our family. My wife and I view digital music players much like a chimpanzee in the wild might view a lava-lamp; as something wonderful and incomprehensible that apparently fell from the sky.

Sam wanted this fascinating device because he loves music. At the ripe age of 11, he's developing his own unique tastes and interests. However, his parent's CD collection is still trapped in the seventies and eighties. 'Look honey, this is a band called Bread! Mama and I love them! You want to listen? Oh, wait, Pat Benatar! She is so cool. And Van Halen, now there's some rock and roll!' Sam humors us, but you can tell he isn't a big fan of the 'oldies.' I mean the classics, no parentheses necessary.

So, given the fact that we are obviously dinosaurs in the music department, Sam wants to listen to more modern bands. Which is fine. Except that it isn't. As times have changed, music has changed. And now, the references to sex, alcohol and drugs; the use of profanity; the discontent, all are more over the top than ever. Admittedly, music is often confrontational. It is an expressive artistic medium that young people have used for ages to share their angst, communicate their desires and annoy every adult around them. It has been that way since the days of harp and lyre.

However, it is no longer encrypted in the codes that we all sat around LP players trying to understand, hoping to unveil by playing backwards. (Listen! I think Gene Simmons said, 'Go, downtown motor-home, buy chicken socks, big lizard, dogs on acid!') Modern pop, rock, country and rap artists have all thrown restraint to the wind and say whatever they would say to anyone from their parents to their friends to their parole officers. This is a problem. (So is the content of videos, but that's another column).

This is a problem because children are little sponges. This is a problem because boys desperately want to use profanity to sound tough even when their parents don't use it. And this is a problem because kids want to be like their idols, who in many cases are entertainers of widely varied talent and intelligence.

So, when musicians are saying things that would cause old ladies to have sudden bleeding out the eyeballs if their hearing aids were working, kids in the pre-teen range want to say them too. And when their idols suggest doing things that would make parents have screaming nightmares, so much the better.

Enter the MP-3 player. With this device, I can select the music that I'm willing to let my child hear, without fear of the ravages of every song on a CD by a particular band. With this device, I can give my son some of the music he wants, while denying him some of the worse lyrics imaginable. Of course, as he ages he'll be able to go to a friend's house and download things I object to; but I can still scroll down his player and find the lyrics on the Internet. Like George W., I have no problem with spying.

I want to protect my kids, because I'm confident that if MTV is any indication, entertainers will keep offering my children rage, frustration, violence and substance abuse. It will keep telling them to disrespect women and have as many sex partners as possible. It will continue shouting that gang life is real life. It will keep offering huge music contracts to people who lack, shall we say, talent.

Words have enormous power. They can fill our children with hope, passion, joy and laughter; they can comfort their pain and help them to handle the frustration of stone-age parents, and hormones that cycle at 10,000Mhz. But words, especially in music, don't have to drag them down or make their troubled years more troubled.

It's our job as parents to protect them. We have to fill their minds with words that will carry them further and higher. We need to shield them from deception masquerading as art. And if protecting them means comprehending the mystery of MP-3 players, well fetch me the manual and my reading glasses. It's going to be a long night.

Snake vs. cats

In a world of sorrow, confusion, strife and the endless nightmare of politics and reality television, it's good to know that for good, clean fun, all you really need is a $5 laser pointer and a cat. Point laser at floor, get cat's attention and voila! Endless fun on four paws. Cats are uniquely qualified for this sort of activity. First, because they can jump, turn, run and climb in ways that make dogs look as agile as boulders. Second, because their little velvet paws aren't equipped for polished hardwood floors. Third, despite all of the people who attribute near psychic intelligence to cats, one fact remains. Cats don't know what laser pointers are. Turn on the pointer and all a cat thinks is 'Red bug, red bug, catch it!'

Of course, it isn't just cats. Not long ago, while demonstrating this wonderful fusion of physics and fur, my four-year-old goddaughter Brianna ran around the corner, saw the dot from the laser and screamed 'what's that?' She and my daughter Elysa spent the next 10 minutes chasing the dot around the house. Not as fast as cats, but equally entertaining. (Little girls also have trouble with hardwood floors).

Elysa and I made another entertaining discovery last week. It started with the remote-control snake that her brother Elijah received for Christmas. Face it, any story that starts with 'remote controlled snake' has to be a good one.

The snake had been unused because it needed batteries. Like many modern toys the screws that hold the battery cover in place were manufactured by tiny fairies, using magic and electron microscopes. It took a while for me to find a screwdriver that would work. Finally, batteries in place, we had a working, pseudo-snake that could move across the floor with the help of four double A's. Elysa and I had an idea. 'Here kitty, kitty!'

Now the snake is a plastic affair in about six segments. It is brown, with white and black circles. It moves in a straight line forward and backward. It can move right or left in a wide arc. The snake is propelled by wheels that are located on its belly. Its eyes, unlike most snakes in nature, are flashing red lights.

Here's the important point: house cats do not know that snakes don't have wheels or flashing red eyes. As far as Felis Domesticus is concerned, all snakes have these items as standard equipment.

As a former student of zoology, and an observer of animals and humans for many years, I am convinced that we have some degree of genetic memory. We may call it instinct, but buried deep in our minds, through some wonder of DNA or folded proteins, we know important things that our ancestors learned the hard way. This holds true for cats as well. Despite wasting their lives eating processed cat food all day (in between multiple power-naps), my cats recognized something primal in the plastic snake.

So when it began to slither/roll toward them with its eyes flashing off and on, the cats' reasoning led them to a simple conclusion. 'Long, brown slithery things have been known to consume cats'. This little primal thought process resulted in Socks the cat suddenly expanding to some four times his original size. From nose to tail, his fur stood on end till his tail looked like a bottle-brush. He never needed a Xanax more in his life. He and his brother Barbie danced around the snake and vaulted straight into the air while we all laughed ourselves breathless.

Let me say, to any animal lover who thinks I'm mean or abusive, I figure our felines owe me. They owe me for the cost of cat-litter and cat-food. And they owe me a little something for all of the nights I have been awakened by cats setting off the burglar alarm by knocking dishes into the floor while playing a midnight game of 'you bite my tail, I'll bite yours'. Besides, if they didn't live in my house, they would probably know first-hand that snakes don't have wheels or flashing eyes.

It was good fun. It doesn't take much. Lasers, children, cats, toys. Life is just full of delightful things to entertain us on the cheap if we only look around. The cats, sadly, now think the snake is passé. Wait a minute...I wonder if Brianna knows that snakes don't have wheels?

Bird Flu

As a young man, I recall very clearly the time my church went through an 'end of time' phase. It was very fashionable in the seventies and eighties, and I still remember posters and billboards advertising 'prophecy meetings' where we would learn more about the imminent arrival (and probably identity) of the anti-Christ, the gory details of persecution that the faithful would endure, and about the time-line within which most of it would happen.

I was deeply affected. Thanks to sermons and tracts, I was convinced that I would endure nuclear war, would not reach adulthood, probably would not reach my teenage years, and most likely would not live on earth long enough to enjoy the singular pleasures of the opposite sex. As a Christian, I would have to endure lots of misery, most likely inflicted by Chinese or Russian communists in their godless crusade to master the world and stamp out all evidence of faith.

Imagine my anxiety! Kept from sex by the devil in league with communists! I mean, I understood a lot of bad things about the devil, and I still have serious issues with collectivism (now more well-informed), but to think that they would conspire to 1) stop me from going to church and 2) interrupt my pursuit girls? Ghastly.

Of course, if I was among the faithful and the timeline was right, I had the rapture to look forward to. The trumpets would sound (or not, depending on who you spoke to), and suddenly all the faithful would be gone. Many a young Christian man and woman like myself woke from a deep nap to find nobody at home, and was convinced they had been 'left behind'. Some ran outside screaming. Some just turned on the television and enjoyed the peace and quiet.

Now, before anyone sends me scripture citations and an invitation to damnation, let me say that I still believe the Bible. I believe in the rapture and the judgment. I believe in the end of all things, and their renewal. I'm more comfortable with them now because I'm secure in my faith; and because I have acquired, over the years, a wife and four children. I now know all about girls, so there's no hurry.

But what I'm saying, in a joking way, is that I worried about a lot of stuff that didn't happen, and didn't foresee a lot of things that did, like tsunamis and hurricanes. There was no nuclear war, the communists are all drinking espresso, worrying about the conservative right, and trying to open convenience stores. And the church is still strong in America and in many other places worldwide.

New enemies and fears have come, and some have gone. Islamic extremists have replaced Mao and Brezhnev (who seemed rational by comparison). The fears of a new ice-age, popular in my youth, have been trumped by fears of global warming. World-wide anthrax and smallpox outbreaks were all the rage not long ago, but have failed to materialize. And meteorites still come close enough to earth to muss up our hair, but haven't stopped season after season of bad television.

Last year we had SARS (Severe Acute Respiratory Syndrome). This year, we have Bird-Flu. And we are all being whipped into a frothing frenzy over what to do. 'Can I eat chicken? Can I pet chickens? Can I watch chickens on movies?' And ultimately, we're overdoing it again. Fear of things we can barely control is something we seem to enjoy almost as much as reality shows. Odd, considering that obesity is killing Americans every day, along with drunk driving and domestic violence. These we can do something about; but they aren't as exciting as assorted potential world-wide disasters.

Certainly bird-flu could be a problem, just as the 1918 flu was, killing millions around the world. But with modern communications, disease surveillance, anti-virals, vaccines and supportive care for complications, it's less likely. Therefore, the one thing we should all do is worry less. A lot less. Because most of the bad things we fear never come to pass.

Our ancestors in the ancient world had worries that were just as real: plague, pestilence, famine, war and even crucifixion for making those testy Romans angry. But what Jesus said then rings as true today as 2000 years ago. 'Who among you, by worrying, can add a single hour to his life?' I'm guessing no one in the audience raised a hand.

Homework Checker

One of the things I hate the very most is checking my children's homework. It's a tragic embarrassment, but sometimes, after I check it, it comes home with red marks where I was wrong. Then, for a few days, I have to avoid eye contact with the teacher who figured out that I didn't, after all, know my multiplication tables.

I spent a lot of time in school. If you add it all up, from first grade to residency, I was in formal education for 23 years. During that time, I learned how to study. In fact, when I decided to go to medical school instead of being a journalist, I had to play 'catch-up' from years of largely ignoring math and science.

My college evenings and weekends were often marathon study sessions, in which I would set the clock in the morning, turn it off for bathroom breaks and food, and study for 8-10 hours. My wife, then girlfriend, was very patient. She tried to coax me to take a break and have some fun. Then, realizing I was dedicated to a romantic day with 'Fessenden and Fessenden's Organic Chemistry text', she would go out with my roommate. I wish I had listened and had a little more fun. Like they did. I'm not bitter, not me, because in the end it worked. My point is that it wasn't easy, but I learned a lot of science and math.

My other point is that I promptly forgot tons of it in medical school, which is a bit more focused on things like leaning the location of the spleen and that little twisty thing in your brain that gives you emotions, recognizing diseases that make body parts fall off and learning how to live on a steady diet of caffeine and cheese crackers while not strangling your annoying classmates.

Fast forward to parenthood. My children are in grades K-4, 1, 3 and 5. They bring home lots of homework. Now, I can handle reading and memorization. I understand how to teach someone to study the important points of a passage. I memorized the structures of lots of chemicals. I memorized far more French words than your average waiter in a South Carolina French Restaurant. I memorized most of those nerves and bones and other disgusting things I sometimes see on Saturday night in the emergency room after someone gets 'field-dressed' in a bar. But the worksheets the kids bring home really get me.

The math worksheets are the worst. The reason I have problems is that, to my mind, the instructions can seem confusing. Well, that and my fundamental problem with basic math. (Don't worry, I know drug doses!) So here's how it might look on a second grade math worksheet:

"Timmy has four oranges, Susan has eight. Rafael took six oranges. Draw a picture of the oranges and write a number sentence to show how many oranges remain. "

OK, sound simple. Buy do the oranges have to be orange? Did Rafael take them from Timmy? If he did, Tim now has negative two oranges and is very confused by now. If he took them from Susan, she has two. If he took them from the collective, are we teaching socialism?

"Draw three squares of different sizes. Color the largest one red, color the smallest one black and color the medium one purple."

Fine. But do they mean red, or maroon? The kids and I disagree. Does it have to be purple, or can it be violet?

"How many numbers are there between 3 and 17?"

Wait. Do they mean whole numbers? Do they mean to include 3 and 17? There are really an almost infinite number of subdivided fractions between those numbers! You can see what I mean.

Still, it gets worse with the children's advancing ages. My 5th grader's sheets are about things like adding and subtracting fractions. I can't remember how to do that! It's too much pressure! He has complex multiplication problems and long division; seemingly endless additions and subtractions. I try so hard not to make a mistake, but sometimes I do.

It's not nearly as embarrassing, however, as when I get in a hurry and miss the simpler sheets of my first-grader. A red mark really hurts after I've signed off on 5-4=3, or 6+16=20 or 7x8=78. Fortunately, he's better at it than I am.

The grammar sheets get me, too. Yes, I'm a writer. But I'm a writer the way some people play the piano without music. I know how it should sound. Somewhere, buried in my brain, is the essence of English grammar. When I make a mistake, it alarms. But I can't tell you any of the details. When my children are dissecting sentences and writing the parts of the sentence over the words, I just look away and pretend not to see it. Then, as I get ready for bed, I say, 'honey, did you check Elijah's English homework? Darn it, neither did I. Will you be a sweetheart and do it in the morning? Thanks! I love you!'

I guess we all come around again. After years of education I'm being humbled by simple instructions and by basic math and English. But it's OK. Because when they get to anatomy and physiology one of these days…oh, who am I kidding. I'll have probably forgotten that too.

Love Your Wife

Our Sunday school class has been in Ephesians these days. It contains one of the most contentious passages in the Bible; contentious, at least, to modern minds. That passage is, 'Wives, submit to your husbands as to the Lord'. Now mind you, it doesn't say 'obey', as many men think. Still, if you want to test your survival skills, slip into a convention of the National Organization of Women, steal the microphone and quote that little snippet. Make sure you're wearing a helmet and a Kevlar vest and that you have on your best running shoes. Cleats might help.

The problem with the passage is not that women disregard it, but that men have for so long abused it. Many a holy, evangelical, Bible-believing, rapture expecting man of God has used Paul's words to explain to his wife that it was his way or no way and that the reason was simply 'God says so!' It's hard to trump God.

The real problem with the passage is that men don't seem to read very far in that chapter. If they did, they'd discover that it says, 'Husbands, love your wives, just as Christ loved the church and gave himself up for her to make her holy, cleansing her by the washing with water through the word, and to present her to himself as a radiant church, without stain or wrinkle or any other blemish, but holy and blameless. In this same way, husbands ought to love their wives as their own bodies. He who loves his wife loves himself. After all, no one ever hated his own body, but he feeds and cares for it, just as Christ does the church—for we are members of his body.'

Yikes! So, let me get this straight, I can't just say 'God says it, woman, now here's how it is' and do what I want? I have to consider how it will affect my...my...wife!? What liberal, feminist pandering, whipped guy wrote that? Oh yeah, Paul, the toughest of the tough. Attacked, arrested, beaten, shipwrecked, executed. What a softy he was!

Later he says again for husbands to love their wives, but for wives to respect their husbands. Maybe Paul knew that men weren't very loveable. Maybe he knew that men crave respect and women affection. But in the end, boys, we're called to a higher standard than our spouses. This is an important point and one we have to teach our sons even as we practice it. I know because after many years in the practice of medicine, I have looked into a lot of faces of a lot of broken women.

They are the sad-eyed, hollow-hearted women of the world. They are expected to do it all, including raise the kids, while their husband works and plays. They are the women whose husbands never have a kind word, a date-night or a sweet gift, but expect pure devotion. Some of them are ignored, some of them are actually beaten, and many are replaced by golf, fishing, NASCAR, careers, alcohol or pornography. Sadly, not a few of these women inhabit the pews of churches here in the buckle of the Bible Belt.

Paul said it clearly. Love your wives like Jesus loved his followers. It's a tall order, but it makes for so much delight when it's done correctly. A woman loved is a woman alive. And I think, though it may sound prideful and vain, that my wife is alive.

It's her birthday. Well, not really. She was born on 29 February, Leap day. I guess marrying me was kind of her destiny. And it was her destiny, or her calling, to teach me lesson after lesson about the power of love, and about the way to make a woman (and subsequently her children) shine with it.

As a young man, I didn't get it. I thought it was all about me. I didn't comprehend marriage, even though I said the vows. But down the years, gently (and sometimes forcefully), she explained to me the way of things. And even as I had my doubts, I listened.

Turns out she was just trying to explain to me what the Bible said all along. She's a keeper, that wife of mine.

So read Ephesians, Chapter 5, my brothers. Read it and realize that giving your wife what she so needs and desires is nothing more than obeying the scriptures. If nothing else gets your attention, maybe that will. Like I said, you can't trump God.

Author Biography

Edwin Leap is a practicing physician and writer. He lives and works in western South Carolina, in the foothills of the Blue Ridge Mountains. He was raised in Huntington, West Virginia, graduated from Barboursville High School and Marshall University, and received his MD from West Virginia University. He completed an emergency medicine residency at Methodist Hospital in Indianapolis, IN.

He is married to Jan Mahon Leap, of Madison, West Virginia. She is the love of his life and his college sweetheart. They have four children, described extensively in the previous pages.

Coming Soon!

God Our Papa

For a very long time, I have heard a quiet suggestion in my heart to write about what my role as a father has taught me about God. It hasn't been a door thumping, waking from sleep kind of thing, but subtle and gentle. And in essence, it says to me 'tell them their father loves them'. I can only use what God has given me: the insights and stories, experiences and knowledge of a parent. These were his gifts to me, and will be my gifts to future readers.

These insights and lessons I share are a sort of a short love letter from God your father. But since my children call me Papa, I think of God that way as well. So my upcoming book is called <u>God Our Papa</u>.

I have been working on this for about a year, and I believe I am nearing the end. God-willing (and I believe he's behind it) it won't be long till it is published.

Printed in the United States
200016BV00007B/43-81/A